Contribution Based Pay

Contribution Based Pay

Tools to Identify, Measure and Reward Performance

Dr. Gwen E. Torkelson

Writers Club Press
San Jose New York Lincoln Shanghai

Contribution Based Pay
Tools to Identify, Measure and Reward Performance

All Rights Reserved © 2001 by Gwen E. Torkelson

No part of this book may be reproduced or transmitted in any form or by any means, graphic, electronic, or mechanical, including photocopying, recording, taping, or by any information storage retrieval system, without the permission in writing from the publisher.

Writers Club Press
an imprint of iUniverse.com, Inc.

For information address:
iUniverse.com, Inc.
5220 S 16th, Ste. 200
Lincoln, NE 68512
www.iuniverse.com

ISBN: 0-595-19282-3

Printed in the United States of America

Dedication

This book is dedicated to my family, who taught me persistence and critical thinking, particularly to my sister Ann, who inspired and critiqued the work, and to my husband, who provided support and encouragement in this endeavor.

EPIGRAPH

What is measured gets done. What is rewarded gets repeated.

CONTENTS

Preface xi
Acknowledgements xiii
Introduction xv
Part 1: Analysis and Design 1
   Step 1: Customers, Products and Services *3*
   Step 2: Contribution Statements *8*
   Step 3: Performance Measures and Targets *15*
   Step 4: Essential Functions and Competencies *27*
   Step 5: Evaluate Knowledge, Skills and Abilities *41*
   Step 6: Define the Knowledge, Skills and Abilities *46*
   Step 7: Establish Base Pay *59*
Part 2: Implementation 67
   Step 1: Staff self-evaluation *69*
   Step 2: Finalize Competency Assessment and Base Pay *74*
   Step 3: Prepare Competency Development Plan *78*
   Step 4: Develop Contribution Plan *81*
   Step 5: Measure Performance *84*
   Step 6: Determine Performance Rewards *86*
Conclusions 89
About the Author 91
Appendix 93

PREFACE

Technological change is having a dramatic impact on the nature of competition and on how work is done. Organizations that maintain a hierarchical structure and traditional methods of job design and compensation will have a hard time competing in the new age. The new competition is focused on speed and flexibility, and hierarchy limits both. Organizations need to empower employees to deliver results that satisfy customers while the transaction is occurring.

The best customer interactions will align customer, employee and organizational goals in a triple-win combination. Employees need both customer and organizational information to be effective in this empowered role. Organizational strategy needs to be aligned with daily, front-line decision making so that choices about how to satisfy customers can be made in the context of the situation and the firm's goals. This book provides a set of tools that managers and human resources professionals can use to create jobs that focus on empowered employee contribution.

Managers or HR professionals who follow the preparation and implementation steps outlined in this book will create an environment where employees are motivated to perform at their highest level of contribution. The agony of the annual performance review will be replaced with self-management, self-responsibility and accountability. The best contributors will reap the most rewards, and those rewards will be the ones most valued by the employee. Employees will also be encouraged to grow and develop their skills so that their organization can readily meet the challenges of today and tomorrow. The methodology is equally useful for teams and individual contributors, and cost-effective to implement.

ACKNOWLEDGEMENTS

I'd like to thank Richard J. Longabaugh for having the courage to implement a new compensation system, and the good people at the Wisconsin Housing and Economic Development Authority who embraced the ideas and methods of this reward system. I'd like to thank Lisa Helmeid and Sue Skinner who gave freely of their time, and Barbara Fetkenhauer, Eric Shupert, Lisa Schmidt, Monica Moschkau and Sue Ruhland who helped refine the work. Credit also is due to my sister Ann, who helped by reviewing and improving the work.

INTRODUCTION

Job Framework

Traditional methods of job design and compensation were well matched with hierarchical organization structures. They were created to handle the mechanistic environment created by the industrial revolution. Thinking and doing were separated, and jobs were organized to take advantage of specialization of labor. The work force of the early 1900's possessed a tremendous work ethic, but often lacked education and communication skills. Simple, repetitive jobs were easy to explain, easy to do, and workers were easy to replace. Our environment, work force and technology have all changed dramatically. Our human resource infrastructure has not kept pace.

Most of our current human resource techniques are oriented toward the most basic motivational needs, such as safety and security, while our increasing standard of living, level of education and capability cause us to seek engagement and fulfillment in our chosen careers. This book provides a new framework for designing and compensating jobs so that our fundamental desires to make a contribution are recognized and rewarded.

In our existing HR systems, jobs are focused on duties and responsibilities. They are activity based while what we really want delivered are results that are customer-focused and help the organization meet its' strategic objectives. The job framework for the third millennium is as follows:

JOB FRAMEWORK

Organization Mission, Strategy	Why
Customer	Who
Contribution (Results)	What, When
Success Measures: Service, Speed, Quality, Cost	How Well

Competencies:
    Knowledge
    Skills
    Abilities
	How

Organizational mission and strategy provide the context in which results can be achieved. This means that the organization needs to provide and communicate a strong foundation, articulating its' mission, values, and strategic vision. Specific, measurable strategic objectives must be developed and used as the basis for determining the results needed from business units. Top-level objectives need to be broad-based and comprehensive enough to provide a basis for establishing measures for teams and individuals within an organization. Once the proper foundation is laid, the steps outlined in Part Two will help you align performance with the strategic direction of the organization.

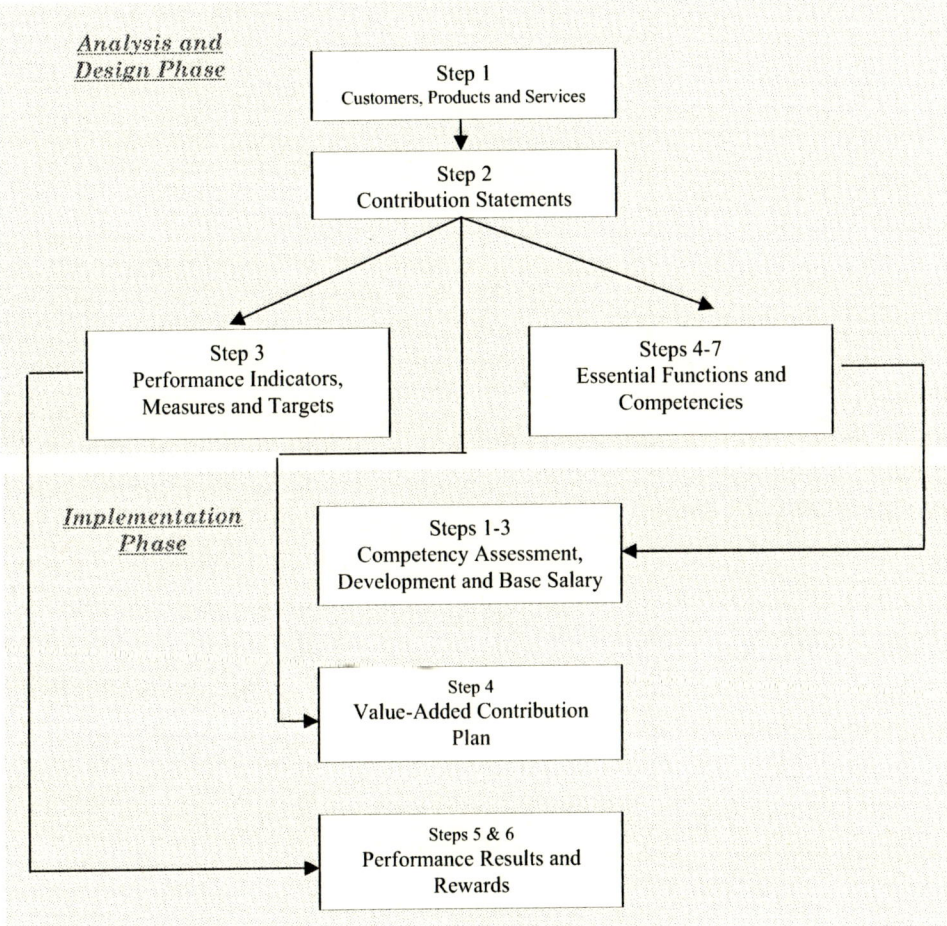

Figure 1: Job Creation Roadmap

Analysis and Design

Procedure Overview

Step

1 Identify the internal and external customers and the products and services each customer expects from the employee (or team).

2 Determine customer requirements for each product or service. These requirements are the contributions the employee (or team) is expected to deliver.

3 Prepare specific measures for each contribution. Critical measures include service, speed, quality and cost. Verify measures with customers and link to organizational strategy.

4 Determine the essential functions and the knowledge, skills and abilities necessary to deliver the contributions.

5 Assess the relative value of each knowledge, skill and ability (KSA). Rate the KSA's with respect to importance, frequency, and development potential.

6 Prepare definitions of each KSA, and develop benchmark behavioral descriptions showing entry, intermediate and advanced level of expertise.

7 Use the essential functions to make external position comparisons to establish the base pay range for the position. Determine the proportion of the salary range attributable to performance and that attributable to KSA's

STEP 1:
CUSTOMERS, PRODUCTS AND SERVICES

What to do:

Identify the internal and external customers and the products and services each customer expects from the employee (or team).

How to do it:

1) Select a position for analysis
2) Recruit several incumbent "job experts" to work with you.
3) Ask the following questions:
    - "What customer groups need your position's products and/or services?"
    - "What products and/or services do you provide to each customer group?"
    - "What do the customer groups use your products and services for?"
    - "What does your position, and the products and services you provide, contribute to the overall success of your company?"

Senior Systems Analyst

- *"What customer groups need your position's products and/or services?"*
  Internal Customers
  >   Customer Service Division Employees
  >   Information Technology Division Colleagues

- *"What products and/or services do you provide to each customer group?"*
  Customer Service Division—Information Systems
  Colleagues—Specifications and mentoring

- *"What do the customer groups use your products and services for?"*
  Customer Service Division—to enter and track orders, issue invoices and answer questions
  Colleagues—to gain information on how to use new tools, new systems-use specifications for coding programs

- *"What does your position, and the products and services you provide, contribute to the overall success of your company?"*
  Clients rethink and improve processes, which improves efficiency by removing unnecessary steps. This improves our reputation with and service to customers.
  Information Systems are fundamental to the operation of the company. The number of customers would preclude the use of manual systems as the sole method of providing service.

Senior Human Resources Representative

- *"What customer groups need your position's products and/or services?"*

    Internal Customers = Field managers

    Direct Supervisor

    Employees

    External = Commercial Clients

- *"What products and/or services do you provide to each customer group?"*

    INTERNAL CLIENTS:

    Field Managers: Hiring staff; recruitment; training hires for first day on the job; providing field managers with expense tracking tools; and acting as the resource for employment laws/regulations/requirements. Acting as communication liaison between the field managers and his supervisor.

    Direct Supervisor: Keeping staffing levels high; preparing contracts for new business; keeping informed as it relates to changes in employment laws/regulations/requirements; to fill-in for other staff during their absence; and to stay on top of and complete administrative responsibilities.

    Employees: Job orientation; to keep supplies they need stocked; payroll; train staff on safety standards; accurate data entry from timesheets and to input their appropriate increases on the system.

    EXTERNAL CLIENTS:

    Consistent service level—dependability; to conduct background checks on staff; to provide sufficient staff; and to complete training before they arrive on site.

- *"What do the customer groups use your products and services for?"*
    Field Managers: Acquire, train and retain staff
    Direct Supervisor: Staffing and administrative services support
    Employees: Orientation, training, payroll
    Commercial Clients: Trained, dependable workers

- *"What does your position, and the products and services you provide, contribute to the overall success of your company?"*
    This position contributes to the overall success of the company by providing the staff to do the labor. Ultimately the position brings higher caliber individuals into the company through appropriate screening and training so that staff is more productive once they get to their assigned job-site. Knowledge of employment/labor laws keeps the company practicing legal employee relations. By developing tools for management to track labor and operating expenses the position is able to help management run the company more efficiently and increase profitability.

Secretary

- *"What customer groups need your position's products and/or services?"*
    Office personnel/employees
    Potential Employees

- *"What products and/or services do you provide to each customer group?"*
    Potential Employees: information and applications
    Office personal/employees: information, supplies, copies, reports, memos, letters, mailings, etc., mailings, etc.

- *"What do the customer groups use your products and services for?"*

    Support to get work accomplished.

- *"What does your position, and the products and services you provide, contribute to the overall success of your company?"*

    If applications were not mailed potential employees would be missed.

    If information or materials are missing or wrong, it can make or break the company. It can set them back considerably.

STEP 2:
CONTRIBUTION STATEMENTS

What to do:

Determine customer requirements for each product or service. These requirements are the contributions the employee (or team) is expected to deliver.

How to do it:

1) Ask the panel of "job experts" to answer the following questions:

    - *"What expectations or requirements do internal or external customers have for each product or service?"*

    - *"How does your customer describe or define a quality product or service?"*

    - *"How will your customers expectations change in the future?"*

2) Use the information provided to develop six to ten Contribution Statements that:

    - Describe end **products or services** the position provides to customers. (Not activities carried out on the job).

    - Specify the critical contributions from the customer's point of view.

- Be sure the statements reflect value-added **results**. Value is added by transforming resources (materials, equipment, intellectual capital) into end products or services. Reviewing work, re-doing work or moving work from one place to another typically do not add value.

3) Check to make sure the contributions encompass all the key aspects of the position. A contribution is considered "key" if it encompasses 5% or more of the total time available for a position during a measurement period.

Senior Systems Analyst

- *"What expectations or requirements do internal or external customers have for each product or service?"*

  Customer Service Division
    - Provide quality product that meets functional needs in a timely fashion.
    - Provide information and advice about state of the art technology options
    - Provide systems that are easy to use (few key strokes, consistent screens)

  Colleagues
    - Specifications
        - Provide detailed specifications for new systems
        - Clearly spell out system objectives
    - Mentoring
        - Provided appropriate level of information and explanation according to individual need/desires
        - Use a sensitive approach to providing information that results in a comfortable relationship

- *"How does your customer describe or define a quality product or service?"*

  Customer Service
    - System works as they have specified, is consistently available and provides predictable results
    - Fast (sub-second) response time when using system

Colleagues
- Specifications
    - Right the first time
    - Clearly written
- Mentoring
    - Knowledge transfer happens—they can proceed on their own
    - They receive accurate information

- *"How will your customers expectations change in the future?"*

    Ease of use will continue to be a key factor—customers will want an increasing level of simplicity

    Increasingly rapid cycle time for development—customers will want new products sooner

    Expert systems will be used more

    Electronic commerce will increase

Contribution Statements:	Percent of time spent
Client information requirements	20%
Computer program designs	20%
Computer system development	20%
Improved systems	15%
Documentation	5%
Trained clients	5%
Trained colleagues	15%

Senior Human Resources Representative

- *"What expectations or requirements do internal or external customers have for each product or service?"*

    Internal Expectations: That accounts are staffed with reliable personnel. That staff will have an understanding of policies and are prepared to start work and have gone through orientation. That payroll is processed accurately. Staff will have the supplies they need to get the job done. Supplies purchased should also be economical. That proposals used to generate new business will be done on a timely basis. That staff development and counseling will be handled at this level. The position is expected to keep the lines of communication with field managers open. The position is expected to provide feedback to his supervisor and field managers.

    External Expectations: That pre-screening of employees is thorough and accurate. That background checks will be completed on all potential employees. That staff will have received OSHA training and other pertinent training. That staff can be trusted in offices unsupervised.

- *"How does your customer describe or define a quality product or service?"*

    Internal Customers

    Fully staffed, high retention of good staff
    Knowledgeable and reliable staff on job sites
    Up-to-date knowledge of procedures and employment laws
    Efficient and cost effective ordering of supplies
    Accurate and fair payroll administration
    Satisfied commercial clients

External Customers

Clean work-sites

Employees that can be trusted

Employees that meet or exceed OSHA standards

- *"How will your customers expectations change in the future?"*

    Customers' expectations will not change much at all in the future. They may adjust slightly with automation and improved cleaning techniques but the majority of their expectations will remain the same.

Contribution Statements:	Percent of time spent
Trained and qualified employees	60%
Delivered staff supplies	20%
Accurate payroll	20%

Secretary

- *What expectations or requirements do internal or external customers have for each product or service?"*

    Correct and timely information

    Correct numbers for billings

- *"How does your customer describe or define a quality product or service?"*

    What is requested is done and sent out on time with all the needed information.

    Questions answered in a timely manner

- *"How will your customers expectations change in the future?"*

    Not a lot of change.

    Expectations will remain providing to the point and all the needed information

Contribution Statements:	Percent of time spent
Human Resource information requirements	70%
Benefits billing statements	20%
Completed clerical work	5%
Informative newsletter	5%

STEP 3:
PERFORMANCE MEASURES AND TARGETS

What to do:

Prepare specific measures for each contribution. Critical measures include service, speed, quality and cost. Verify measures with customers and link to organizational strategy.

How to do it:

1) For each contribution statement, ask the panel of job experts:
   - *"What performance indicators are most critical to meeting customer requirements?"*
     - Have them consider all of the following indicators:

Service	Speed
Quality	Cost
Quantity	Timeliness
Consistency	Productivity
Flexibility	Satisfaction

     - Select the 3 most important indicators for each contribution statement

2) Determine specific numeric or descriptive measures for each contribution.
   - For each indicator selected above, ask:

- "What could be used to measure this indicator? And "In what units?" (e.g. # errors, % completed, $ cost, etc)
- If a qualitative judgment must be made ask: "Who evaluates this part of the job?" "When this person assesses the product or service, what factors should be evaluated?"

3) Create **Baseline** performance targets for each measure:
- For numeric measures use current average performance. Do not set the baseline below the worst performance for any previous period.
- For descriptive measures determine what the judge would see that meant that expectations had been met.
- For cost measures determine the acceptable cost.
- For cost reduction measures consider what amount of rework or waste is acceptable.
- For timeliness measures determine when the project needs to be completed.
- For speed measures determine how fast the cycle time should be.

4) Create **Competitive** level performance targets. These targets are short-term performance improvement goals. They should be set higher than the current average or typical performance, but not higher than the best performance ever achieved.

5) Create **Optimal** level performance targets. These are long-term performance improvement goals. They are significantly better than current performance, and may be the ultimate level of performance, such as zero errors, or 100% satisfaction.

6) Verify the performance measures with representatives from each group of customers to determine if the measures are on target. Make any necessary adjustments.

7) Departments, Division, Business Units and the Organization as a whole often have identified a series of strategic or operational objectives, along with measures to determine if the objectives are met. Meeting organizational objectives and measures depends on the performance of individuals within the organization. Compare the performance measures for this position with the appropriate (department, division, unit, etc.) organizational measures and determine how performance on each contribution helps meet organizational objectives.

Senior Systems Analyst

Performance Indicators

Contribution Statement	Indicator 1	Indicator 2	Indicator 3
Client information requirements	Speed	Quality	
Computer program designs	Speed	Quality	Satisfaction
Computer system development	Speed	Quality	Satisfaction
Improved Systems	Speed	Cost	Quality
Documentation	Consistency	Quality	
Trained clients	Timeliness	Service	Quality
Trained colleagues	Timeliness	Service	Quality

Performance Indicators and Specific Measures

Contribution Statement: Client information requirements

Indicator	Measure/Evaluator	Units/Factors
Speed	Cycle time	Actual to estimate
Quality	Customer Review	Result compared to input

Contribution Statement: Computer program designs

Indicator	Measure/Evaluator	Units/Factors
Speed	Cycle time	Actual to estimate
Quality	Customer	Acceptance criteria
Satisfaction	Customer	% Satisfaction

Contribution Statement: Computer system development

Indicator	Measure/Evaluator	Units/Factors
Speed	Cycle time	Actual to estimate
Quality	Customer	Acceptance criteria
Satisfaction	Customer	% Satisfaction

Contribution Statement: Improved Systems

Indicator	Measure/Evaluator	Units/Factors
Speed	Cycle time	Actual to estimate
Cost	Cost Benefit	Payback period
Quality	Customer	Project justification criteria

Contribution Statement: Documentation

Indicator	Measure/Evaluator	Units/Factors
Consistency	Peer review	Key items present
Quality	Peer review	Accuracy

Contribution Statement: Trained Clients

Indicator	Measure/Evaluator	Units/Factors
Timeliness	Just-in-time training	Proximity to implementation
Service	Questions Answered	Customer survey Repeat inquiries
Quality	Customer Number of questions	Self-sufficiency Help desk calls

Contribution Statement: Trained Colleagues

Indicator	Measure/Evaluator	Units/Factors
Timeliness	Turnaround time	Hours
Service	Questions Answered	Survey
Quality	Customer Training time	Self-sufficiency Hours

Performance Targets

Contribution Statement	Indicator	Measure	Performance Targets
Senior Systems Analyst			
Client information requirements	Speed	Cycle time	**Baseline:** Actual time within 50%-150% of estimate
			Competitive: Actual time within 75% - 125% of estimate
			Optimal: Actual time within 90% - 110% of estimate
	Quality	Review team	**Baseline:** Analyst gains team approval after 5 or 6 review process iterations
			Competitive: Approval after 3 or 4 iterations
			Optimal: Approval after 1 or 2 iterations
Computer program designs	Speed	Cycle time	**Baseline:** Actual time within 50%-150% of estimate
			Competitive: Actual time within 75% - 125% of estimate
			Optimal: Actual time within 90% - 110% of estimate.
	Quality	Customer evaluation	**Baseline:** Several changes required to meet acceptance criteria
			Competitive: Few, minor changes required to meet criteria
			Optimal: Acceptance criteria fully met.
	Satisfaction	Customer evaluation	**Baseline:** 80-85% Customer satisfaction rating
			Competitive: 85-95% Customer satisfaction rating
			Optimal: Above 95% Customer satisfaction rating
Computer system development	Speed	Cycle time	**Baseline:** Actual time within 50%-150% of estimate
			Competitive: Actual time within 75% - 125% of estimate
			Optimal: Actual time within 90% - 110% of estimate
	Quality	Customer evaluation	**Baseline:** Several changes required to meet acceptance criteria
			Competitive: Few, minor changes required to meet criteria
			Optimal: Acceptance criteria fully met.

Contribution Statement **Senior Systems Analyst**	Indicator	Measure	Performance Targets
Computer system development	Satisfaction	Customer evaluation	**Baseline:** 80-85% Customer satisfaction rating
			Competitive: 85-95% Customer satisfaction rating
			Optimal: Above 95% Customer satisfaction rating
Improved Systems	Speed	Cycle time	**Baseline:** Actual time within 50%-150% of estimate
			Competitive: Actual time within 75% - 125% of estimate
			Optimal: Actual time within 90% - 110% of estimate
	Cost	Cost/Benefit	**Baseline:** Payback period two years or more
			Competitive: Payback period one to two years
			Optimal: Payback period one year or less
	Quality	Customer evaluation	**Baseline:** 80-85% Customer satisfaction rating
			Competitive: 85-95% Customer satisfaction rating
			Optimal: Above 95% Customer satisfaction rating
Documentation	Consistency	Peer review	**Baseline:** Rating of 3 on 5 point scale for adherence to standards
			Competitive: Rating of 4 on 5 point scale for adherence to standards
			Optimal: Rating of 5 on 5 point scale for adherence to standards
	Quality	Peer review	**Baseline:** Documentation complete and 100% accurate
			Competitive: Documentation thorough and clear as well as complete and accurate.
			Optimal: Documentation exceptionally helpful in addition to meeting other standards.
Trained Clients and Colleagues	Timeliness	Training Schedule	**Baseline:** Training held 2 to 3 weeks before implementation
			Competitive: Training held 1 to 2 weeks before implementation
			Optimal: Training held within 1 week of implementation

Contribution Statement **Senior Systems Analyst**	Indicator	Measure	Performance Targets
Trained Clients and Colleagues	Service	Question repeats	**Baseline:** Question repeated 4 or more times
			Competitive: Question repeated 2 or 3 times
			Optimal: First answer fully understood
Trained Clients	Quality	Customer evaluation	**Baseline:** 75 - 80% Good to Excellent ratings
			Competitive: 81-90% Good to Excellent ratings
			Optimal: 91%+ Good to Excellent ratings
Trained Colleagues	Timeliness	Turnaround time	**Baseline:** Response to question in 3 to 4 hours
			Competitive: Response to question in 1 to 2 hours
			Optimal: Response to question in less than 1 hour
	Service	Question answered	**Baseline:** Question repeated 4 or more times
			Competitive: Question repeated 2 or 3 times
			Optimal: First answer fully understood
	Quality	Customer evaluation	**Baseline:** 80 – 85% rating of self-sufficiency on topic after training
			Competitive: 86 – 90% rating of self-sufficiency
			Optimal: 91%+ rating of self-sufficiency after training

Business Unit Objectives	Related Performance Target(s)
Customer satisfaction	Program design; System development – satisfaction rating
Quality System	Customer evaluation of all contributions
Timeliness	Information requirements, systems development – cycle time; trained clients and colleagues – turnaround time
Cost Efficiency	Documentation – accuracy; Improved Systems – cost benefit

Senior Human Resources Representative

Performance Indicators

Contribution Statement	Indicator 1	Indicator 2	Indicator 3
Trained and qualified employees	Quality	Timeliness	Consistency
Delivered staff supplies	Timeliness	Cost	Flexibility
Accurate payroll	Quality	Timeliness	Satisfaction

Performance Indicators and Specific Measures

Contribution Statement: Trained and qualified employees

Indicator	Measure/Evaluator	Units/Factors
Quality	Monthly client evaluations/clients	% of completion of specifications
Timeliness	Open positions/supervisor	% of open positions
Consistency	Weekly open position status/supervisor	Results from the open positions study done above. Historic comparison and evaluation.

Contribution Statement: Delivered staff supplies

Indicator	Measure/Evaluator	Units/Factors
Timeliness	All supplies delivered on time/field managers	% of missed items/% of items not ordered.
Cost	Quality products at the best price/supervisor and the budget totals	Amount of money saved over time (budget results).
Flexibility	Meet changing needs of field managers, clients and regulations/Field managers and clients	The appropriate product meets the requirements or needs of clients, field managers, and regulatory guidelines.

Contribution Statement: Accurate payroll

Indicator	Measure/Evaluator	Units/Factors
Quality	Accuracy of data/staff feedback.	Payroll errors
Timeliness	Finishing all payroll adjustments by the payroll deadline/supervisor	Payroll deadline
Satisfaction	Accurate and updated information provided consistently/supervisor.	Legal regulations/historical review of work

Performance Targets

Contribution Statement **Senior Human Resources Representative**	Indicator	Measure	Performance Targets
Trained and qualified employees	Quality	Monthly client evaluations	**Baseline:** Expectations are clear to staff. Staff possesses adequate job knowledge and skill. Staff performs work in satisfactory manner.
			Competitive: Expectations are clear to staff. Staff possesses slightly advanced job knowledge and skill. Staff retention levels are higher than average. Staff performs work in satisfactory manner and even at times surpasses expectations of the client.
			Optimal: Expectations are clear to staff. Staff possesses highly advanced job knowledge and skill. Staff retention remains at an all time high. Staff performs work in a manner that surpasses the expectations of the client.
Trained and qualified staff	Timeliness	Open positions	**Baseline:** Weekly open position rate of $\leq 5\%$.
			Competitive: Weekly open position rate of $\leq 3\%$.
			Optimal: Weekly open position rate of $\leq 1\%$.
	Consistency	Weekly open position status	**Baseline:** Monthly open position rate of $\leq 5\%$.
			Competitive: Monthly open position rate of $\leq 3\%$.
			Optimal: Monthly open position rate of $\leq 1\%$.
Delivered staff supplies	Timeliness	All supplies delivered on time	**Baseline:** Accounts run with $\leq .5\%$ margin of error in supply stock missing/not ordered.
			Competitive: Accounts run with $\leq .25\%$ margin of error
			Optimal: Accounts run with a full stock of the right supplies all of the time.
	Cost	Quality products at the best price	**Baseline:** Total costs stay within budget.
			Competitive: Total costs stay within budget or below budget figures.
			Optimal: Total costs stay below budget figures

	Flexibility	Meet changing needs	**Baseline:** Uses appropriate vendor 95% of the time.
			Competitive: Appropriate vendor is used 98% of the time.
			Optimal: Appropriate vendor is used all of the time.
Accurate payroll	Quality	Accuracy of date	**Baseline:** 1% error rate
			Competitive: .5% error rate
			Optimal: 0% error rate.
	Timeliness	Adjustments completed by deadline	**Baseline:** Deadline met 97.5% of the time.
			Competitive: Deadline met 99% of the time
			Optimal: Deadline met 100% of the time.
	Consistency	Accurate and updated information provided over time	**Baseline:** .5% error rate over time.
			Competitive: .25% error rate over time.
			Optimal: 0% error rate over time.

STEP 4:
ESSENTIAL FUNCTIONS AND COMPETENCIES

What to do:

Determine the essential functions and the competencies necessary to deliver the contributions.

How to do it:

1) Functions are the tasks we do in order to accomplish the contributions expected from the position. **Essential functions** represent a summary of the key tasks associated with a job, and are common to all job description formats. Essential functions are used to comply with the Americans with Disabilities Act and will be used in a later step to make market salary comparisons. The essential functions are those duties that *must* be performed in the job.

   a) Review each contribution statement and determine what must be done on the job to produce the results required by customers. List the appropriate function after each contribution statement.

   b) Determine which functions are essential. Ask the following questions:

   - *"Does the position exist to perform this function?"* For example, when a person is hired to microfilm documents, the ability to operate a microfilm camera is an essential function because this is the key reason for the job.

- *"Is the function highly specialized?"* In highly skilled positions, a worker is hired because they possess special expertise in a particular area. The performance of that specialized task would be an essential function.
- *"Are there a limited number of employees among whom the function can be distributed?"* In this type of situation, functions may become essential that might not be considered essential if there were a larger staff where the work can be more spread out.
- *"Would the job be fundamentally altered if you were to remove the function in question?"* *If the purpose of the job would still be accomplished without performing the function, it might not be an essential one.*
- *"What happens if the function is not performed?"* *If there are no particular consequences for failure to perform the function it might not be essential.*

2) Competencies are composed of the underlying knowledge, abilities and skills needed to perform the work that generates results and contributions. As employees increase their competency level, they are more easily able to achieve better results. In addition, increasing competencies helps position the organization to readily adapt in a rapidly changing environment. Growing competencies in a flat organization provides a sense of upward mobility and career development, which aids in retention of growth-motivated staff.

   a) Determine the **Knowledge** necessary to accomplish each contribution statement:

   Knowledge is defined as a body of information applied directly to the performance of a function.

   - Ask the following questions:

- "What subject matter areas are covered by this contribution?"
- "With what facts or principles must the worker have an acquaintance or understand in these subject areas?"
- Examples of knowledge statements:

    Knowledge of accounting principles, practices and procedures

    Knowledge of computer science theory and concepts

    Knowledge of management principles, practices and procedures

b) Determine the **Abilities** necessary to accomplish each contribution statement:

Ability is defined as a present competence to perform an observable behavior or a behavior that results in an observable product.

- Ask the following questions:
    - "What is the nature and level of language ability, written or oral, required of the worker on the job?" "Are there complex oral or written ideas involved in performing the contribution, or will simple instructional materials suffice?"
    - "What mathematical ability must the worker have?" "Will the incumbent use simple arithmetic, complex algebra?"
    - "What reasoning or problem solving ability must the worker have?"
    - "What instructions must the worker follow?" "Are they simple, detailed, involved, abstract?"
    - "What interpersonal abilities are required?" "What supervisory or managerial abilities are required?"
    - "What physical abilities such as strength, coordination, visual acuity must the worker have?"
- Examples of ability statements:

    Ability to research, evaluate and make recommendations

Ability to conduct training

Ability to design and write programs in "C"

Ability to design software programs to solve business problems

c) Determine the Skills necessary to accomplish each contribution statement:

Skill is defined as a present, observable competence to perform physical activities associated with mental processes.

- Ask the following questions:
    - *"What activities must the worker perform with ease and precision?"*
    - *"What are the manual skills that are required to operate machines, vehicles, equipment or to use tools?"*
- Examples of Skill statements:

Skill in the use of a calculator

Skill in the use of standard tools and equipment

Skill in the use of keyboards

Senior Systems Analyst

Contributions, Tasks, Essential Functions and Competencies

Contribution Statement: Client information requirements

Task	Essential Function?
Meet with clients to identify need	Yes
Analyze needs	Yes
Develop data model	Yes
Document findings	No

Knowledge	Ability	Skill
Business knowledge	Conduct interviews	Keyboarding
System development methodology	Make presentations	Calculator
Systems analysis	Communicate technical information to laymen	
Structured programming	Communicate in oral and written forms	
System platform	Research and analysis	
	Use software tools	

Contribution Statement: Computer program designs

Task	Essential Function?
Develop specifications	Yes
Identify inputs/outputs	Yes
Design system flow and interaction	Yes
Design user interface	Yes
Identify security requirements	No
Develop object model	Yes

Knowledge	Ability	Skill
Systems design	Logically analyze information	Keyboarding
Security standards	Be creative	
Structured programming	See the big picture	
	Work with details	
	Research information	
	Communicate in writing	
	Use software tools	

Contribution Statement: Computer system development

Task	Essential Function?
Write code	Yes
Evaluate code	No
Test code	Yes
Implement code	No

Knowledge	Ability	Skill
Business knowledge	Be creative	Keyboarding
Structured programming	Work with details	
Test plan development	Code	
Implementation procedure	Test software	
Operating system	Use software tools	
System development methodology	Communicate in writing	
Project management		

Contribution Statement: Improved Systems

Task	Essential Function?
Determine changes needed	Yes
Code changes	Yes
Test changes	Yes
Implement changes	No

Knowledge	Ability	Skill
System knowledge	Identify problem and solution	Keyboarding
Structured programming	Write code	
Implementation procedures	Test software	
Operating system	Use change management software	
Business knowledge	Communicate in writing	

Contribution Statement: Documentation

Task	Essential Function?
Review system code	No
Write documentation	No

Knowledge	Ability	Skill
System knowledge	Communicate in writing	Keyboarding
Documentation standards	Use software tools	

Contribution Statement: Trained Clients

Task	Essential Function?
Present system change	Yes
Discuss inter-relationships with other systems	Yes
Answer questions	Yes

Knowledge	Ability	Skill
System knowledge	Communicate orally and in writing	Audio-visual equipment
System platform	Establish effective working relationships	
Business knowledge	Communicate technical information to laymen	

Contribution Statement: Trained Colleagues

Task	Essential Function?
Communicate to understand problem	Yes
Identify problem	Yes
Identify the solution	Yes
Communicate solution	Yes

Knowledge	Ability	Skill
System knowledge	Communicate orally and in writing	
Systems analysis	Establish effective working relationships	
Computer system design	Identify problems and solutions	
Division policies and procedures		
System platform		

Secretary

Contributions, Tasks, Essential Functiosns and Competencies

Contribution Statement: Human Resource Information Requirements

Task	Essential Function?
Copying (most confidential info)	Yes
Setting up meetings and/or luncheons	Yes
Distributing Applications	Yes
Contacting branch offices with questions and/or answers	Yes
EEO Filing	Yes
Salary/Job information correct in HRIS system	Yes
Emergency contact information entered	Yes
Offer letters processed	Yes
Process COBRA packs for terminated or retired employees	Yes

Knowledge	Ability	Skill
Basic office procedures	To maintain discretion when dealing with internal and external customers	Computer skills Word, Excel, PowerPoint
Of company policies	Manage multiple priorities	
Of employees names and locations	Communicate effectively	
	To work under pressure	
	To work unsupervised	
	To set-up meetings/ luncheons in multiple locations	
	To handle confidential items	

Contribution Statement: Benefits billing statements

Task	Essential Function?
Enter new employee information	Yes
Coding out billings	Yes
Timely processing	Yes
Delete information of terminated employees	Yes

Knowledge	Ability	Skill
Basic accounting	To meet deadlines	Computer skills excel/word
Benefits programs	To work unsupervised	Calculator usage
	To handle confidential materials	
	To organize materials	
	To be punctual	

Contribution Statement: Completed clerical work

Task	Essential Function?
Copying	Yes
Data entry and/or typing	Yes
Follow written instructions	Yes

Knowledge	Ability	Skill
Basic office procedures	Manage multiple priorities	Computer skills Excel Word
Office Machines	Communicate effectively	
Office policies	To work under pressure	
	To work unsupervised	
	To handle confidential items	

Contribution Statement: Informative Newsletter

Task	Essential Function?
Data entry	Yes
Data collection	Yes
Copy/Fold/Stuff Newsletter	Yes
Compile data for entry	Yes
Ensure data received is correct	Yes

Knowledge	Ability	Skill
Company and surrounding office (for articles)	Proofreading	Computer skills: Publisher
Knowledge of office machines (copier, folder, etc.)	Editing	
	Work unsupervised	

Senior Human Resources Representative

Contributions, Tasks, Essential Functions and Competencies

Contribution Statement: Trained and qualified employees

Task	Essential Function?
Recruiting	Yes
Interviewing	Yes
Training/Orientation	Yes
Pre-Screening	Yes
Follow-up with field managers on staff quality to heighten awareness of what they need in a staff person.	No
Career development/counseling of staff	No

Knowledge	Ability	Skill
Interviewing Methods	To make decisions and recommendations	Telephone
Training Methods	To conduct training	Computer
Pre-Screening Requirements	To be able to ask the right questions of candidates and their former employers	
Coaching Methods	Guide staff and act as a resource for staff and management	
Company Policies	Communication Skills	
	Documentation	

Contribution Statement: Delivered staff supplies

Task	Essential Function?
Maintain an effective inventory system	Yes
Shop different vendors to find/ensure economical product is being used.	Yes
Keep yourself educated/up-to-date on OSHA standards to make sure supplies meet regulations.	Yes
Maintain a reliable delivery system of the supplies.	Yes
Review the budget on a regular basis to see if supply costs are in line.	No

Knowledge	Ability	Skill
Comparison Pricing	To negotiate	Telephone
OSHA Regulations	Communication Skills	Computer
Computer Programs	Research products and pricing	Calculator
Financial Principles	Maintain spreadsheets	
Budgeting/Accounting Principles	Realize effects of pricing on budget	
Profitability Strategies		

Contribution Statement: Accurate Payroll

Task	Essential Function?
Remain knowledgeable and up-to-date on employment regulations and company policies as they relate to payroll.	Yes
Become familiar with each staff person's wage requirements.	Yes
Enter data correctly on the payroll system/have a sound knowledge base of the payroll system. Know how to make corrections.	Yes
Implement a proofing system of some sort to spot inaccurate data entry.	No

Knowledge	Ability	Skill
Regulations	Interpret Data (Research and learn regulations on an on-going basis)	Data entry
Individual Staff's Wage Information	Reading	Computer
Computer Payroll Software		

STEP 5:
EVALUATE KNOWLEDGE, SKILLS AND ABILITIES

What to do:

Assess the relative value of each knowledge, skill and ability. Rate the KSA's with respect to importance, frequency, and development potential.

How to do it:

Use the guide presented under each category to identify the appropriate level of each Knowledge, Skill or Ability necessary for effective performance.

1) Importance: *"How important is this KSA to effective performance?"*

Minimal Importance		Moderate Importance		Major Importance
1	2	3	4	5

2) Development potential: *"To what extent will increased expertise make a significant difference in performance?"*

Minimal Difference		Moderate Difference		Major Difference
1	2	3	4	5

3) Frequency: *"How often is this KSA used in delivering effective performance?"*

Yearly	Twice Yearly	Monthly	Weekly	Daily	Hourly	Continually
1	2	3	4	5	6	7

Example

Knowledge, Skill, Ability	Importance	Development Potential	Frequency
Knowledge of computer science theory and concepts	4	2	7
Ability to conduct training	2	4	3
Skill in the use of keyboards	5	1	7

Senior Systems Analyst

Knowledge (K), Skill (S), Ability (A)	Importance	Development Potential	Frequency	Total
K1 Business knowledge	4	4	7	15
K2 Systems development methodology	4	4	7	15
K3 Systems analysis	4	4	7	15
K4 Structured programming	4	4	5	13
K5 System platform	4	4	5	13
K6 Systems design	4	4	7	15
K7 Security standards	3	2	2	7
K8 System knowledge	4	5	5	14
K9 Implementation procedures	4	4	2	10
K10 Operating system	4	4	5	13
K11 Documentation standards	3	3	3	9
K12 Test plan development	4	4	2	10
K13 Project management	4	4	5	13
K14 Policies and procedures	4	3	5	12
A1 Conduct interviews	4	4	4	12
A2 Make presentations	4	4	3	11
A3 Communicate technical information to laymen	4	4	4	12
A4 Communicate in oral and written forms	5	4	7	16
A5 Research and analysis	4	4	4	12
A6 Use software tools	4	3	4	11
A7 Use logic in analysis	5	5	7	17
A8 Be creative	4	4	5	13
A9 See the big picture	5	3	3	11
A10 Work with details	5	4	5	14
A11 Write code	4	4	5	13
A12 Test software	4	4	4	12
A13 Identify problems and solutions	4	4	5	13
A14 Effective relationships	4	4	5	13
S1 Keyboarding	3	2	7	12
S2 Calculator	3	2	4	9
S3 Audio-visual equipment	2	2	2	6

Secretary

Knowledge, Skill, Ability	Importance	Development Potential	Frequency	Total
Basic office procedures	4	5	7	16
Knowledge of company policies	4	5	7	16
Know employees names & locations	4	3	7	14
Basic accounting	3	3	4	10
Benefits programs	4	5	7	16
Office machines	5	4	7	16
Company happenings in surrounding offices	4	3	5	12
Maintain discretion when dealing with internal or external customers	5	5	5	15
Manage multiple priorities	5	5	7	17
Communicate effectively	5	5	7	17
Meet deadlines	5	5	5	15
Work unsupervised	4	5	5	14
Handle confidential material	5	5	5	15
Work under pressure	5	5	4	14
Proofreading	4	3	5	12
Editing	4	3	3	10
Setting up meetings	4	3	3	10
Computer skills: Excel Word Publisher	5	5	7	17
Interpersonal skills	5	5	7	17
Time management	5	5	7	17
Organization	5	5	7	17
Use of a calculator	3	3	3	9
Punctuality	5	5	5	15
			Total	344

Senior Human Resource Representative

Knowledge, Skill, Ability	Importance	Development Potential	Frequency	Total
K-Interviewing Methods	5	5	5	15
K-Training Methods	4	4	5	13
K-Pre-Screening Requirements	4	4	5	13
K-Coaching Methods	4	5	5	14
K-Company Policies	5	4	5	14
K-Comparison Pricing	4	4	4	12
K-OSHA Regulations	5	5	3	13
K-Profitability Strategies	4	4	4	12
K-Regulations	5	5	4	14
K-Individual Staff's Wage Information	5	4	4	13
K-Computer Payroll Software	4	4	5	13
A-To make decisions and recommendations	5	4	7	16
A-To conduct training	4	4	5	13
A-To be able to ask the right questions of candidates and their former employers	3	4	6	13
A-Guide staff and act as a resource for staff and management	5	4	7	16
A-Communication Skills	5	5	7	17
A-Documentation	5	4	5	14
A-To Negotiate	3	4	3	10
A-Research products and pricing	3	3	3	9
A-Maintain spreadsheets	4	3	5	12
A-Realize effects of pricing on budget	4	4	4	12
A-Interpret Data (Research and learn regulations on an on-going basis)	4	4	4	12
A-Data entry	4	4	4	12
S-Telephone	4	4	7	15
S-Computer	5	4	7	16
S-Calculator	3	3	4	10
S-Reading	4	3	7	14

STEP 6:
DEFINE THE KNOWLEDGE, SKILLS AND ABILITIES

What to do:

Prepare definitions of each KSA, and develop benchmark behavioral descriptions showing entry, intermediate and advanced level of expertise.

How to do it:

1) Determine the domain of the KSA. The domain indicates the scope of the Knowledge, Skill or Ability required by the position under review. For example, a Technical Specialist and a Database Administrator both need to possess knowledge of computer networking, testing and system administration. The domain of the knowledge is different as shown below:

Domain

Knowledge	Technical Specialist	Database Administrator
Computer networking, testing and system administration	Computer connectivity, including cabling, disk and CPU usage, UNIX system commands, troubleshooting errors	Database structure, concepts, software testing methodology, system security issues

2) Write behavioral descriptions that illustrate how a particular Knowledge, Skill or Ability is demonstrated on the job. Develop

benchmarks for individuals just starting out in a position, individuals who have gained experience and expertise to support independent work, and lastly, individuals who are acknowledged experts and idea leaders.

Individuals possess entry-level KSA's when they

- Work under the supervision and direction of a more experienced staff member
- Work products are a portion of a larger project or activity being overseen by an experienced staff member
- Lack experience and status in the organization
- Are expected to willingly accept supervision and direction
- Do most of the detailed and routine work on a project
- Exercise guided creativity and limited initiative
- Are learning to perform well and accomplish a task within the time allowed.

Individuals possess intermediate-level KSA's when they

- Go into depth in one problem or technical area
- Assume responsibility for a definable portion of a project, process or clients
- Work independently and produce significant results
- Develop credibility and a solid reputation
- Rely less on manager for answers and develops own resources to solve problems
- Increase in confidence and ability

Individuals possess advanced-level KSA's when they:

- ❏ Make significant contributions in own area of expertise but also contribute in other key areas
- ❏ Stimulate others by sharing ideas and information
- ❏ Help develop expertise in other staff members through leadership and mentoring roles
- ❏ Represent the organization to individuals and institutions outside the organization
- ❏ Negotiate and make commitments for the organization

Example

KSA	Domain	Entry	Intermediate	Advanced
Ability to conduct training	Subject knowledge, presentation skills, adult training techniques, facilitation techniques, composure, credibility	Prepares and presents small group training on familiar and basic processes using established materials. Evaluations indicate room for growth	Prepares and presents large group training and training on more complex subjects. Regularly receives good evaluation ratings from participants	Able to independently prepare and present any type of scheduled or spontaneous training. Consistently receives excellent ratings from participants.
Ability to research, evaluate and make recommendations	Collecting appropriate material, qualitative and quantitative analysis, report preparation	Researches generally available information and uses it for analysis. Recommendations are logical based on alternatives	Increased depth of analysis and wider search for supporting information. Sound, logically supported recommendations	Highest quality research and analysis involving complex topics requiring sophisticated techniques
Knowledge of computer applications	Software capabilities, options and use	Understands functionality of basic office suite applications.	Understands functionality of wide range of applications. Provides support to others	Acknowledged expert on many packages. Regularly resolves difficult problems
Knowledge of accounting principles, practices and procedures	Financial statements, chart of accounts, profit and loss statement, budgets, ledgers, trending analysis	Basic understanding of accounting principles. Reviews financial statements, chart of accounts, profit and loss statement with some direction. Discovers weaknesses in operations and applies corrective measures without direction	Regularly reviews financial statements, budgets, operating accounts, chart of accounts. Ascertains compliance with GAAP. Demonstrates knowledge of customers business and makes recommendations for improving financial record keeping	Performs complex computations, trending analysis and assesses financial capacity by reviewing records and accounting procedures of customers. Knowledgeable of GAAP and ensures that customers are in compliance. Understands and conducts audits

Senior Systems Analyst

Competency	Domain	Entry	Intermediate	Advanced
K1 Business Knowledge	Goals, procedures and work flow of the business unit	Basic familiarity gathered through review of documentation and discussion.	Considerable familiarity gained through work on several related projects	Thorough familiarity gained through in-depth exposure gained over a sustained period of time working on all aspects of the system.
K2 Systems development methodology	Internal policies and procedures relating to computer system development	Understands basic concepts and methodology	Understands how to apply methodology to systems projects	Thorough understanding of methodology. Suggests changes as new techniques emerge.
K3 Systems analysis	Principles, practices and procedures involved in analyzing business processes to create and improve efficiency of work flow	Understands basic concepts and methodology. Can independently analyze projects of limited complexity	Understands how to apply concepts and methods to a wide variety of projects. Works independently	Innovates based on breadth of knowledge. Provides guidance to others and leads team for complex, critical projects
K4 Structured programming	Concepts, techniques and application of specific languages	Working knowledge of two languages	Working knowledge of one language, expert knowledge of one language	Expert knowledge of two or more languages
K5 System platform	Hardware and system software used to house a project	Basic knowledge of small systems that do not cross platforms	Considerable knowledge — can integrate systems across platforms	Expert knowledge — can accommodate remote processing and complex interfaces
K6 Systems design	Concepts relating to system flow, user interface design, database structure and objects	Basic understanding of design concepts. Can design small systems (< 6 weeks development time) independently	Can design medium systems (6 weeks to 4 months development time) independently and large systems as a member of a team	Oversees work of system design teams dealing with large, complex systems. Mentors others.
K7 Security standards	Internal policies and procedures relating to system security	General familiarity with procedures and ability to find necessary information	In-depth understanding of procedures. Can independently apply standards	Thorough understanding of procedures and related issues. Can develop new standards. Mentors others

Competency	Domain	Entry	Intermediate	Advanced
K8 System knowledge	Software capabilities and options	Understands basic functionality of specific system.	General familiarity with several systems.	Thorough knowledge of functionality for most systems
K9 Implementation procedures	Internal policies and procedures for moving systems from development to production environments	General familiarity with procedures and ability to find necessary information	In-depth understanding gained through experience. Can independently use procedures	Thorough understanding of procedures and related issues. Can develop new procedures and train others
K10 Operating system	Commands, syntax, functions and directory structure	Knowledge of basic UNIX commands. Able to use VI editor	Intermediate commands and system functions. Uses makefiles and produces C-shell programs	Produces more complex C-Shell programs and makefiles; familiarity with file systems and connectivity issues
K11 Documentation standards	Internal policies and procedures detailing format and contents of system documentation	General familiarity with procedures and ability to find necessary information	In-depth understanding of procedures. Can independently apply standards	Thorough understanding of procedures and related issues. Can develop new standards and train others
K12 Test plan development	Phases, steps and procedures in checking a system for conformance to specifications	General familiarity with procedures and ability to find information. May need assistance in testing systems.	In-depth understanding with procedures. Can independently apply steps to moderately complex systems.	Thorough understanding of procedures and related issues. Directs testing of major projects.
K13 Project management	Planning and applying a methodology to a specific project in order to reach the desired outcome.	Basic knowledge of project management for small, limited scope projects	Ability to apply knowledge of project management to all projects	Knowledge applied to large, complex projects and transfers of knowledge to project leaders
K14 Policies and procedures	Operating policies within and across functional areas	General familiarity with procedures and ability to find necessary information	In-depth knowledge in specific area and closely related areas	In-depth knowledge across functional areas
A1 Conduct interviews	Asks appropriate questions, seeks clarification, achieves understanding	Needs some guidance and assistance in obtaining information through interviews	Independently obtains information from customers through interviews	Provides assistance to others in obtaining information through interviews.

Competency	Domain	Entry	Intermediate	Advanced
A2 Make presentations	Public speaking to small and large groups along with preparing necessary information, visual aids and collateral materials.	Can prepare for and make easily understood presentations to small groups about familiar topics. Asks for assistance if needed	Presentations are effective, address the topic, meet the needs of the target audience, creative in expression, uses visual aids to add interest	Communicates in a manner that provides for understanding of complex topics. Can comfortably make well-received presentations to very large groups.
A3 Communicate technical information to laymen	Understand and translate technical jargon into clear, concise, non-technical language	Translates and explains computer acronyms and application program logic	Explains relational database structures, other file structures and processes to acquire data for reporting or inquiry	Clearly explains complex technical processes and application interfaces in an understandable way
A4 Communicate in oral and written forms	Quality of interaction through written documents (memos, letters, reports, forms, e-mail) or dialogue (meetings, telephone conversations, voice-mail)	Needs some guidance and assistance in communication to generate clear, accurate and easily understood messages	Independently provides correct and clear communication, enhances accuracy through use of tools, advice and practice	Communications are clear, concise, accurate and at the appropriate level; versatile, creative in expression; enhances understanding of complex topics. Provides help to others
A5 Research and analysis	Collect appropriate information, review facts and figures, examine and organize the information in order to develop a plan or solution	Researches generally available information and uses this as a basis for analysis. Minimal guidance is required for moderately complex projects.	Increased depth of analysis and wider search for supporting information. Sound, logically supported recommendations. Independent work on complex projects	Highest quality research and analysis involving complex topics requiring sophisticated techniques. Designs and monitors work of colleagues
A6 Use software tools	Accessing and using specific computer applications for completing work	Basic level of proficiency in using system. Some assistance needed.	Intermediate level of proficiency in using system. No assistance needed for day-to-day tasks	Advanced level of proficiency in using system. Provides assistance to others on complex issues
A7 Use logic in analysis	Systematic manner of thinking in approach to problems	Capable of handling recurring, normal situations; analyzes results, recommends changes	Thought process is clear and reasonable in deriving a decision or action in relatively complex situations. Beginning to anticipate future requirements.	Thought process is systematic and justified to support non-routine situations, develops new and effective approaches to unfamiliar situations

Competency	Domain	Entry	Intermediate	Advanced
A8 Be creative	Identify new and innovative ideas, procedures or processes.	Can offer suggestions for minor improvement to existing systems.	Offers suggestions for major improvements to existing systems.	Proposes new systems to solve emerging business problems
A9 See the big picture	Consider the long-term impact of actions on the system as a whole	Understands part of the system but needs assistance to relate to the system as a whole	Wider understanding of components allowing for independent work on projects with limited scope	Broad understanding of system components and interactions. Able to assist others in determining impact of changes. Able to see where system needs to go in next 3 to 5 years.
A10 Work with details	Thoroughness and precision in designing a solution to a business problem	Solution responds to key business issues in an acceptable manner	Solution provides functionality beyond that which is immediately identified	Solution solves existing problem, adds functionality and resolves related but unidentified issues. System has hooks for anticipated future development.
A11 Write code	Translate computer specifications into a computer program using the appropriate programming language	Ability to modify existing code, create new code or add new functionality for small projects of limited scope. Adheres to standards	Independently modifies code, creates code or adds functionality for larger, more complex projects. Codes interfaces to other systems	Directs and reviews work of others on complex projects. Codes very complex, critical systems.
A12 Test software	Generate test data and use it to determine if software is functioning properly	Works with small systems with a limited number of variables and simple routines	Works with systems with a moderate number of variables and routines of moderate complexity	Works with very large, complex systems using key data
A13 Identify problems and solutions	Define problems, isolate causes, identify remedies and take or recommend action	Clearly defines problems, accurately identifies causes, develops several possible solutions, determines and documents the best course of action and implements or recommends the solution	In addition to entry-level abilities, is able to lead others through the problem solving cycle, providing guidance and direction to a team, or can solve more complex problems.	Is able to foresee problems, identify critical issues, bases options on effectiveness, resolves complex problems through mediation, negotiation and collaboration. Forestalls problems through effective planning and foresight.

Competency	Domain	Entry	Intermediate	Advanced
A14 Establish and maintain effective working relationships	Elicits cooperation and support from clients and co-workers	Handles normal relationships is an acceptable manner. Has some difficulty with complex relationships	Experienced in handling all situations in a professional manner	Can handle any relationship. Regularly called upon to assist in more challenging situations
S1 Keyboarding	Touch typing, using keypad and mouse	Accurate touch typing at a slow speed, uses mouse	Uses special function keys, accurate typing at moderate speeds	Thoroughly familiar with all functions, accurate typing at fast speeds
S2 Calculator	Using keypad and functions	Able to obtain accurate results at a slow pace. Understands regularly used functions	Able to obtain accurate results at a moderate pace. Understands and can use all but the most complex functions	Able to obtain accurate results at a fast pace. Understands and uses complex operations correctly
S3 Audio-visual equipment	Operating media used in making presentations	Needs guidance and assistance in setting up and using audio-visual equipment	Able to set up and use standard overhead projector, PC viewer	Able to independently set up and use all types of multi-media equipment

Senior Human Resources Representative —Key Competencies Only

Competency	Domain	Entry	Intermediate	Advanced
Interviewing Methods	Elicit information to determine qualifications for screening decisions	Sit-in on interviews led by experienced staff, give feedback to interviewer after the meeting, take notes and learn from experienced staff.	Conduct initial interview and bring forward top candidates for a second interview with more experienced staff.	Conduct interview and select most qualified candidates, and train entry-level interviewers.
Training Methods	Facilitating staff on-the-job and classroom training	Review training tools and information so that you can teach the information effectively; work directly with supervisor on developing training sessions; attend training as a spectator.	Take control of a large portion of the training session. Investigate current/new techniques for presenting data.	Conducts training of new staff independently, develops new techniques and ideas to improve training, shares ideas with other training staff.
Pre-Screening Requirements	Following proper procedures in regards to background checks and investigation of prospective staff.	Review and learn what regulations need to be followed; understand importance of pre-screening process; review client expectations. Conduct initial pre-screening and review with supervisor.	Investigate potential staff. Independently follow correct and current procedures. Report results to supervisor or client.	Conduct pre-screening, follow-up with client and staff, make appropriate decisions regarding results of the pre-screening, and supervise entry-level staff. Act as a resource for staff on how and why this needs to be done
Coaching Methods	Provide staff with constructive feedback on their performance	Entry-level staff will need to heavily rely on their supervisor for direction and feedback on coaching techniques. Role-play situations before working directly with staff. Document results of coaching sessions and analyze how they went. Read books on different coaching methods and perspectives.	Be able to handle most coaching opportunities independently. Solicit feedback from direct supervisor as to how the coaching session went, what you might have done differently, and how the employee will benefit from your intervention. Read/research different coaching methods.	Provide coaching to the coaches. Create tools that will help other managers coach more efficiently, keep them informed, and organized. Provide on the spot feedback to employees and provide a good example to other coaches.

Competency	Domain	Entry	Intermediate	Advanced
Company Policies	Practical interpretation of company guidelines and policies to staff and management.	To study the policy manual and commit to memory the important aspects of each policy and how they relate to day-to-day work or certain key situations. Refer to the policy manual when working with staff. Learn how to use the manual effectively and efficiently.	Being able to realize when a policy should come into play. To have created an organized means of being able to quickly reference pertinent sections of the policy manual. To act as a resource to non-human resource staff regarding policy and how to carry it out.	To work on policy changes and implementation of those changes. To be able to recognize the need for a change and how to make the changes to policy. To posses the knowledge to make independent decisions regarding the appropriateness of a policy. To act as a resource to all staff on policy.
To make decisions and recommendations	To be able to act independently on behalf of the company with regard to candidates for hire, supply issues, areas of the business that are tied to regulatory statues, etc.	To be able to draw conclusions as to appropriate courses of action. To work directly with your supervisor or co-workers before taking independent action to make sure that your ideas are in line with departmental objectives.	To be able to act independently on behalf of your supervisor. To coach entry-level staff and review decisions with them in order to better prepare them for this responsibility.	To be able to make decisions on behalf of the company. To help coach all staff and provide clear direction and expectations up-front. To enable other staff to make well informed decisions.
Guide staff and act as a resource for staff and management	To hold a thorough understanding of regulations, policy, and the role of human resources so that you can act as a resource on these areas for other staff in the company.	To research and study pertinent regulations. To hold a degree in human resources related field of study or possess at least two years previous work related experience. To study company policy.	To keep current on regulations and policy updates. To provide managers and staff with training and updates on regulations and policy. To make yourself available to managers and staff in order to provide them with guidance and accurate information as it relates to these topics.	To conduct research and surveys so that you can analyze policy and make/recommend necessary or important changes. To keep current on regulations and be able to make staff aware of updates. To act as a resource for your immediate staff as well as others in the company. To be considered the company expert in these areas

Competency	Domain	Entry	Intermediate	Advanced
Communication Skills	To be able to effectively present your ideas. To be able to negotiate with peers and clients. To use proper vocabulary. Listening and paraphrasing skills	To work directly with your supervisor or co-workers before taking independent action to make sure that your ideas are in line with departmental objectives. It will be helpful if the candidate has taken a speech class.	To be able to act on behalf of your supervisor and in their absence. To be able to clearly express thoughts and ideas as they relate to your expertise and company strategies. To be able to make presentations to prospective clients. Independently conduct interviews.	To act as a spokesman for the company. To coach others about effective communication techniques. To educate staff about their role as representatives of the company. To be the media contact for the company.
Computer Skills	A thorough understanding of programs, i.e., Word, Excel, PowerPoint. Efficient keyboarding skills. To be able to use software and shortcuts efficiently to create spreadsheets and presentations.	If candidate has not had 1-2 years of experience working heavily with Office products further training/course work will be required. Staff will work independently with computer and software. A thorough understanding of short cuts and presentation capabilities/techniques will be required.	To stay current as new software and office products are introduced. To use the system efficiently and effectively without asking for assistance.	To know office products and upgrades well enough to teach others about efficiencies. To stay current as new software and office products are introduced. To use system efficiently and effectively without asking for assistance.

Secretary—Key competencies only

Competency	Domain	Entry	Intermediate	Advanced
Work unsupervised	Working on one's own-without being watched over.	Be able to be shown a task and complete it without supervision.	Be able to begin projects on your own.	Be able to find work and begin projects without asking- make personal judgment decisions.
Communicate effectively	Conveying messages and information to others in a way that they can understand.	Be able to ask questions and speak to internal personnel in a clear manner.	Some external customers, employee contact, as well as internal.	Able to explain policies/procedures to internal as well as external customers. Clear and exact information.
Computer Skills/Knowledge	Working with computers and knowing different programs and their capabilities of them.	Basic knowledge of Word and Excel programs.	Know how to move around documents – use command keys.	Know Word and Excel in depth, ability to help or train others with problems.
Work under pressure	Having the ability to focus on your work several projects and deadlines at one time	Able to handle several assignments (given by one supervisor).	Handle several tasks- (prioritize) as well as work for multiple people.	Handle internal and external phone calls and questions, while keeping workload up to date. Handle several supervisors.
Handle confidential material	Knowing what materials are confidential and having the ability to keep them confidential. Using discretion.	Phone calls of a private nature- handle confidentially	Handle confidential materials pertaining to legal or family matters	Handling of confidential employees' files and telephone conversations. Drug screen test results.
Organization/ multiple priorities	Calculating which tasks should come first and how to see it through.	Have a clean work area-uncluttered.	May have 2 or more jobs to complete in a day. Prioritize accordingly.	Have a filing system set for each supervisor for incomplete tasks and for completed tasks or in process tasks. Know what is due when.
Office procedures	Basic operations of office are known and understood.	Be familiar with people in office and basic office structure.	Know title of employees and have a general feel of their duties.	Know specific job titles and duties, not only of those in home office but in field offices as well.

Step 7: Establish Base Pay

What to do:

Use the essential functions to make external position comparisons to establish the base pay range for the position. Determine the proportion of the salary range attributable to performance and that attributable to KSA's

How to do it:

1) Determine if you wish to conduct your own survey or use existing survey material. This process assumes the use of published survey data.

   Determine the market area for your positions. Market areas may be local, statewide, regional, or national. Markets are likely to vary for positions, with higher level or more technical positions drawing from a larger market area.

   Visit the library to determine what survey data is readily available. Call trade associations, professional societies and government agencies for additional survey resources. Evaluate the resources for applicability to your situation: Determine:

   ❑ *If any of your former employees left your firm to work for other companies that have participated in the survey.*

   ❑ *If you have hired many employees from the participating companies*

   ❑ *If the survey covers at least some firms that are regarded as competitors.*

   ❑ *If the survey covers companies of similar size to your firm.*

- ❑ *If the survey covers jobs similar to those in your firm.*
- ❑ *If the survey data is dominated by a few particularly high- or low-paying firms.*

Your aim is to select surveys of competitive companies within a relevant geographic area.

2) Review the data that is presented in the survey to ascertain that the rates of pay are clearly defined. Base rates of pay should not include shift differentials, overtime rates or other premium rates.

3) Select the jobs in the survey that are similar to those in the firm. To do this, study the brief job descriptions provided with the survey, and compare these brief descriptions to the essential functions you identified in Step 3.

4) Find the average wage for each job from the survey. The best measure to use is the inter-quartile range, or the middle 50 percent, which is the range of data resulting from discarding the highest 25 percent and the lowest 25 percent of the reported data. The exclusion of the high and low quartiles eliminates from the data trainees and persons who are overpaid, and reduces the mean's sensitivity to extremes. If the inter-quartile range is not available, use the mean.

5) Once you have identified the market wage for each position, you may want to update the information by increasing the data by making a cost of living adjustment based on the change in the Consumer Price Index since the time the data was published.

6) Base salary data reported in surveys factors in pay for performance. When paying for contributions, you want base salary to only reflect the core competencies possessed by staff. Therefore, you need to subtract from the market wage an amount that accounts for performance pay.

Use your performance appraisal system or judgment to determine:

- *Which employees are "superior" performers, defined as those whose performance is better than 85% of their colleagues, and only 15% turn in better performance.*
- *Which employees are "average" performers*
- *Which employees are "low performing" employees, defined as those employees whose performance is less effective than 85% of their colleagues, and only 15% turn in worse performance.*

Obtain salary data for employees in each category for each position.

- Calculate an average salary for each category.
- Find the difference between the mean "superior" performer category and the "average" performer category.
- Find the difference between the mean "low performing" category and the "average" performer category.
- Calculate the average of these two differences. This is the performance differential paid in your company.
- Subtract the performance differential from the market wage to establish the competency-based average salary
- Establish the salary range by alternately adding and subtracting 10% to 25% (depending on your firms past practice for salary administration) to and from the average wage.

Senior Systems Analyst

Senior Systems Analyst (1997 Wage Data)	# of observations	Annual Salary
	2	$18,720
	7	22,880
	4	27,040
	9	31,200
	12	35,360
	33	39,520
	73	46,800
	43	52,000+

Total observations = 183

Eliminate observations from the 46 lowest and 46 highest salaries:

Remaining data:	# of observations	Annual Salary
	21	$39,520
	70	46,800

Mean market wage = $45,120

Performance Category	Salary	Average
Superior		48,367
S. Skinner		48,500
L. Helmeid		47,000
C. Johnson		49,600

Average	**43,417**
K. Smith	44,500
L. Larsen	43,000
B. Margenau	42,750
Low	**38,600**
T. Andre	38,250
J. Jackson	37,750
G. Baker	39,800

Existing Pay for Performance Differential

Superior – Average Differential	Average – Low Differential	Overall Average Performance Differential
$48,367 – $43,417 = $4,950	$43,417 – $38,600 = $4,817	$4,884

Competency-Based Average Salary:
(Market Wage—Performance Differential)
 $45,120—$4,884 = **$40,236**

Senior Systems Analyst Salary range: $32,200 - $48,300

Senior Human Resource Representative

# Of Incumbents	Minimum Salary	Average Salary	Maximum Salary
2	$40,161	**$41,431**	$42,701
6	$37,621	**$38,891**	$40,160
14	$30,000	**$31,270**	$32,540
17	$35,081	**$36,351**	$37,620
19	$32,541	**$33,811**	$35,080
Total Observations = 58			

After eliminating 15 from the lowest and 15 from the highest salaries:

Remaining data: # of Incumbents =
    17          $36,351
    19          $33,811

Mean market wage = $35,081
Performance Differential = $7,016
Range: $28,065 - $42,097

Secretary

Observations	Salary
326	20376
923	22673
698	25850
852	27586
523	28895

Total Observations: 2851

Remaining data:

536	22673
698	25850
662	27586

Mean market wage: $25558
Performance Differential: $5,191
Range: $20,367- $30,749

IMPLEMENTATION

Procedure Overview

Step 1   Staff conducts self-evaluation of competencies using definitions and benchmarks. Level of attainment is indicated along with supporting rationale.

Step 2   Evaluation is discussed with coach or team members to finalize competency assessment. Base salary is determined using competency assessment.

Step 3   Competency development plan is prepared indicating tasks, projects or training activities proposed for the upcoming year. The competencies slated for development are selected based on organizational strategy and enhancing core competencies.

Step 4   Quarterly contribution plan is developed for current processes and projects, including performance measures for service, speed, quality and cost as defined above. Value-added contribution is determined for each item.

Step 5   System for regularly collecting performance data for each contribution is implemented. System provides direct feedback on results to employee (or team).

Step 6   Performance and Development activities are tracked and evaluated as they occur throughout the year. Evaluation includes a full-circle assessment. Rewards, *StaffShare Reward Units* (SRU)©, are earned based on successful performance and value-added contribution. Staff determines how the reward will be delivered—e.g., cash, time-off, added benefits, etc

STEP 1: STAFF SELF-EVALUATION

What to do:

Staff conducts self-evaluation of competencies using definitions and benchmarks. Level of attainment is indicated along with supporting rationale.

How to do it:

1) Prepare and distribute an evaluation form to each staff member.
2) Provide competency descriptions prepared in Step 6 above for use in conducting the evaluation.

Senior Systems Analyst

Employee Name:

Competency	Use Competency definitions to determine your level for each item. Check your position on the continuum.	Support your rating by providing specific examples of training, experience, or experience. Expand on the reverse if necessary.
K1 Business knowledge	Entry Intermediate Advanced 1 2 3 4 5 6 7 8 9 10 √ (at 5)	Six years experience working on numerous systems projects for key customer
K2 Systems development methodology	Entry Intermediate Advanced 1 2 3 4 5 6 7 8 9 10 √ (at 5)	Attended internal training. 6 years experience using methodology to complete work
K3 Systems analysis	Entry Intermediate Advanced 1 2 3 4 5 6 7 8 9 10 √ (at 6)	College course work supplemented by two external seminars and work experience
K4 Structured programming	Entry Intermediate Advanced 1 2 3 4 5 6 7 8 9 10 √ (at 6)	College course work supplemented by annual training and 12 years work experience
K5 System platform	Entry Intermediate Advanced 1 2 3 4 5 6 7 8 9 10 √ (at 5)	3 years experience with new platform. Supported by annual vendor training programs
K6 Systems design	Entry Intermediate Advanced 1 2 3 4 5 6 7 8 9 10 √ (at 5)	College course work supplemented by two external seminars and work experience
K7 Security standards	Entry Intermediate Advanced 1 2 3 4 5 6 7 8 9 10 √ (at 6)	Attended internal training. 12 years experience using standards in programming work
K8 System knowledge	Entry Intermediate Advanced 1 2 3 4 5 6 7 8 9 10 √ (at 5)	6 years working on systems for key customer
K9 Implementation procedures	Entry Intermediate Advanced 1 2 3 4 5 6 7 8 9 10 √ (at 7)	12 years on-the-job experience.
K10 Operating system	Entry Intermediate Advanced 1 2 3 4 5 6 7 8 9 10 √ (at 5)	3 years experience with new system, supplemented by vendor training
K11 Documentation standards	Entry Intermediate Advanced 1 2 3 4 5 6 7 8 9 10 √ (at 8)	12 years on-the-job experience. Helped write current standards. Approve work of others
K12 Test plan development	Entry Intermediate Advanced 1 2 3 4 5 6 7 8 9 10 √ (at 7)	College course work plus 12 years OJT experience. Review and approve plans for other staff
K13 Project management	Entry Intermediate Advanced 1 2 3 4 5 6 7 8 9 10 √ (at 7)	Two external seminars on project management. Software training. PM on 6 large projects
K14 Policies and procedures	Entry Intermediate Advanced 1 2 3 4 5 6 7 8 9 10 √ (at 8)	Staff member for 12 years. Experienced in all areas, provide training to new staff
A1 Conduct interviews	Entry Intermediate Advanced 1 2 3 4 5 6 7 8 9 10 √ (at 5)	External training program on interviewing skills. 6 years experience. Good customer comments

Skill	Level	Comments
A2 Make presentations	Entry 1 2 3 Intermediate 4 5 6 7√ Advanced 8 9 10	External training program. Positive customer comments.
A3 Communicate technical information to laymen	Entry 1 2 3 Intermediate 4 5 6 7√ Advanced 8 9 10	Customer comments sometimes indicate confusion over terminology
A4 Communicate in oral and written forms	Entry 1 2 3 Intermediate 4 5√ 6 7 Advanced 8 9 10	Writing could be developed. Work regularly revised by supervisor
A5 Research and analysis	Entry 1 2 3 Intermediate 4 5 6 7 Advanced 8 9√ 10	Thoroughly understand all systems due to work in all areas through rotation
A6 Use software tools	Entry 1 2 3 Intermediate 4 5 6 7 Advanced 8√ 9 10	Vendor training and regular experience with most tools
A7 Use logic in analysis	Entry 1 2 3 Intermediate 4 5 6 7 Advanced 8 9√ 10	Peer review of code receives highest rating
A8 Be creative	Entry 1 2 3 Intermediate 4 5 6 7√ Advanced 8 9 10	Customer and colleague feedback indicate positive comments in this area
A9 See the big picture	Entry 1 2 3 Intermediate 4 5 6 7√ Advanced 8 9 10	Supervisor and customer feedback indicate skill in this area
A10 Work with details	Entry 1 2 3 Intermediate 4 5 6 7√ Advanced 8 9 10	Systems regularly receive positive comments from customers on thoroughness
A11 Write code	Entry 1 2 3 Intermediate 4 5 6 7 Advanced 8 9√ 10	Generally programs and specifications are bug-free in few iterations
A12 Test software	Entry 1 2 3 Intermediate 4 5 6 7 Advanced 8√ 9 10	12 years work experience.
A13 Identify problems and solutions	Entry 1 2 3 Intermediate 4 5 6 7√ Advanced 8 9 10	Problem-solving seminar. 6 years work experience in systems
A14 Effective relationships	Entry 1 2 3 Intermediate 4 5 6√ 7 Advanced 8 9 10	Customer comments generally favorable. Development possible
S1 Keyboarding	Entry 1 2 3 Intermediate 4 5 6 7 Advanced 8 9 10	Good speed, very high accuracy.
S2 Calculator	Entry 1 2 3 Intermediate 4 5 6 7 Advanced 8 9√ 10	Completely comfortable with job use.
S3 Audio-visual equipment	Entry 1 2√ 3 Intermediate 4 5 6 7 Advanced 8 9 10	Need help setting this up. Can use it once it's ready.

Senior Human Resource Representative

Competency	Use Competency definitions to determine your level for each item. Check your position on the continuum.	Support your rating by providing specific examples of training, experience, or experience. Expand on the reverse if necessary.
K1 Interviewing methods	Entry Intermediate Advanced 1 2 3 4 5 6 7 8 **9** 10	Six years experience in recruitment and selection
K2 Training methods	Entry Intermediate Advanced 1 2 3 **4** 5 6 7 8 9 10	Internal training program supplemented by 4 years experience
K3 Pre-screening requirements	Entry Intermediate Advanced 1 2 3 4 5 6 **7** 8 9 10	Course in job analysis, 3 years conducting job studies
K4 Coaching methods	Entry Intermediate Advanced 1 2 3 4 **5** 6 7 8 9 10	In-house training, six months experience
K5 Company policies	Entry Intermediate Advanced 1 2 3 4 5 6 **7** 8 9 10	9 years experience with current employer
K6 Comparison Pricing	Entry Intermediate Advanced 1 2 3 4 5 6 **7** 8 9 10	4 years purchasing experience
K7 OSHA Regulations	Entry Intermediate Advanced 1 2 3 4 5 6 **7** 8 9 10	Training seminars and on-the-job experience, 2 years
K8 Payroll Software	Entry Intermediate Advanced 1 2 3 4 5 6 7 **8** 9 10	3 years experience with new system, supplemented by vendor training
A1 Make decisions and recommendations	Entry Intermediate Advanced 1 2 3 4 5 6 7 8 9 **10**	Very few instances of changes in decisions by supervisors.
A2 Conduct training	Entry Intermediate Advanced 1 2 3 4 5 **6** 7 8 9 10	Positive evaluations from staff. Some comments for improvement
A3 Ask right questions of candidates and former employers	Entry Intermediate Advanced 1 2 3 4 5 6 7 8 **9** 10	High level of success in providing staff who stay on the job
A4 Guide staff and act as a resource for staff and management	Entry Intermediate Advanced 1 2 3 4 5 6 7 8 **9** 10	Positive comments from staff, continuing reliance by management
A5 Communicate in writing and orally	Entry Intermediate Advanced 1 2 3 4 **5** 6 7 8 9 10	Oral presentations could be improved. Written work fine
A6 Prepare documentation	Entry Intermediate Advanced 1 2 3 4 5 6 **7** 8 9 10	Documentation has supported employer in all challenged cases
A7 Negotiation	Entry Intermediate Advanced 1 2 3 4 5 6 **7** 8 9 10	Favorable pricing obtained for several products
A8 Research products and pricing	Entry Intermediate Advanced 1 2 3 4 5 6 **7** 8 9 10	Research provided support for negotiations
A9 Maintain spreadsheets	Entry Intermediate Advanced 1 2 3 4 5 6 **7** 8 9 10	Keep data, but weak on graphing and reporting skills
A10 Interpret data	Entry Intermediate Advanced 1 2 3 4 **5** 6 7 8 9 10	Several position papers adopted by senior management
S Telephone	Entry Intermediate Advanced 1 2 3 4 5 6 **7** 8 9 10	Acceptable level for job requirements

S Calculator	Entry Intermediate Advanced 1 2 3 4 5 6 7 8 9 10 √	Acceptable level for job requirements
S Computer	Entry Intermediate Advanced 1 2 3 4 5 6 7 8 9 10 √	Good keying speed, high accuracy

STEP 2:
FINALIZE COMPETENCY ASSESSMENT AND BASE PAY

What to do:

Evaluation is discussed with coach or team members to finalize competency assessment. Base salary is determined using competency assessment.

How to do it:

1) Supervisor completes form for each staff member.
2) Supervisor compares own form with form submitted by staff member.
3) Supervisor prepares new form considering information received from staff member.
4) Supervisor schedules meeting with staff member to discuss and agree upon assessment.
5) Supervisor calculates a point value for each competency by multiplying the assessment percent with the relative value of the competency determined in Part 3, Step 5. (See below)
6) Supervisor adds all point values together and divides by the total points possible to determine a base salary percent. (See below)

| Total possible points = 381 | Assessment points = 296 | Base salary percent = 78% |

7) Subtract the minimum salary from the maximum salary. Multiply the result by the base salary percent. Add the result to the minimum salary to determine base salary amount.

Salary Range: $32,200—$48,300

Maximum Salary:	$48,300
Minimum Salary	- 32,200
Difference	16,100
Base Salary Percent	x 78%
Result	$ 12,558
Minimum Salary	+ 32,200
Base Salary Amount	$ 44,758

Senior Systems Analyst

Knowledge (K), Skill (S), Ability (A)	Assessment	Percent Score	Relative Value	Total
K1 Business knowledge	Intermediate	70%	15	10.5
K2 Systems development methodology	Intermediate	50%	15	7.5
K3 Systems analysis	Intermediate	75%	15	11.25
K4 Structured programming	Intermediate	75%	13	9.75
K5 System platform	Intermediate	75%	13	9.75
K6 Systems design	Intermediate	75%	15	11.25
K7 Security standards	Intermediate	70%	7	4.9
K8 System knowledge	Intermediate	70%	14	9.8
K9 Implementation procedures	Advanced	100%	10	10
K10 Operating system	Intermediate	55%	13	7.15
K11 Documentation standards	Advanced	100%	9	9
K12 Test plan development	Advanced	100%	10	10
K13 Project management	Advanced	85%	13	11.05
K14 Policies and procedures	Advanced	100%	12	12
A1 Conduct interviews	Intermediate	70%	12	8.4
A2 Make presentations	Intermediate	70%	11	7.7
A3 Communicate technical information to laymen	Intermediate	60%	12	7.2
A4 Communicate in oral and written forms	Intermediate	55%	16	8.8
A5 Research and analysis	Advanced	100%	12	12
A6 Use software tools	Advanced	95%	11	10.45
A7 Use logic in analysis	Advanced	90%	17	15.3
A8 Be creative	Intermediate	75%	13	9.75
A9 See the big picture	Intermediate	75%	11	8.25
A10 Work with details	Intermediate	75%	14	10.5
A11 Write code	Advanced	100%	13	13
A12 Test software	Advanced	95%	12	11.4
A13 Identify problems and solutions	Intermediate	75%	13	9.75
A14 Effective relationships	Intermediate	55%	13	7.15
S1 Keyboarding	Advanced	95%	12	11.4
S2 Calculator	Advanced	100%	9	9
S3 Audio-visual equipment	Entry	35%	6	2.1
Totals			381	296.05

Senior Human Resources Representative

Knowledge (K), Skill (S), Ability (A)	Assessment	Percent Score	Relative Value	Total
K1 Interviewing methods	Intermediate	70%	15	10.5
K2 Training methods	Intermediate	50%	13	6.5
K3 Pre-screening requirements	Intermediate	75%	13	9.75
K4 Coaching methods	Entry	25%	14	3.5
K5 Company policies	Intermediate	75%	14	10.5
K6 Comparison Pricing	Intermediate	75%	12	9.0
K7 OSHA Regulations	Intermediate	70%	13	9.1
K8 Payroll Software	Intermediate	70%	13	9.1
A1 Make decisions and recommendations	Advanced	100%	16	16
A2 Conduct training	Intermediate	55%	13	6.5
A3 Ask right questions of candidates and former employers	Advanced	100%	13	13
A4 Guide staff and act as a resource for staff and management	Advanced	100%	16	16
A5 Communicate in writing and orally	Intermediate	55%	17	9.35
A6 Prepare documentation	Advanced	95%	14	13.3
A7 Negotiation	Intermediate	70%	10	7
A8 Research products and pricing	Intermediate	70%	9	6.3
A9 Maintain spreadsheets	Intermediate	70%	12	8.4
A10 Interpret data	Advanced	70%	12	8.4
S Telephone	Intermediate	75%	15	11.25
S Calculator	Intermediate	75%	10	7.5
S Computer	Intermediate	75%	16	12
Totals			280	202.95

| Total possible points = 280 | Assessment points = 202.95 | Base salary percent = 72% |

Salary Range: $28,065—$42,097

Maximum Salary:	$42,097
Minimum Salary	- 28,065
Difference	14,032
Base Salary Percent	x 72%
Result	$ 10,103
Minimum Salary	+ 28,065
Base Salary Amount	$ 38,168

STEP 3:
PREPARE COMPETENCY DEVELOPMENT PLAN

What to do:

Competency development plan is prepared indicating tasks, projects or training activities proposed for the upcoming year. The competencies slated for development are selected based on organizational strategy and enhancing core competencies.

How to do it:

1) Review organizational and department objectives for upcoming year.
2) Review competency assessment for each staff member
3) Determine which areas for improvement will provide the most return for effort employed.
4) Select the competencies for development
5) Identify specific work projects or training opportunities for development.
6) Prepare training plan.

Senior Systems Analyst

Business Unit Objectives	Competency Improvement Areas
Customer satisfaction	Communication Effective relationships Business knowledge
Quality System	Business knowledge Systems development methodology Operating System
Timeliness	Systems development methodology Business knowledge Systems analysis Systems design
Cost Efficiency	Systems development methodology Business knowledge Systems analysis Systems design

Training Plan

Competency Improvement Areas	Training Plan
Communication	Attend intensive workshop on effective communication skills for technical staff
Effective relationships	Perceptive Communications training
Business knowledge	Serve four week internship with major customer
Operating System	Attend operating system training
Systems development methodology	On-the-job training
Systems analysis	Attend advanced analysis course
Systems design	Attend advanced design course

Senior Human Resource Representative

Business Objectives	Competency Improvement Areas
Customer satisfaction	Communication Coaching Methods Training Methods
Timeliness	Interviewing Methods Pre-screening requirements
Cost Efficiency	Comparison Pricing Negotiation

Training Plan

Competency Improvement Areas	Training Plan
Communication	Attend workshop on effective presentation skills
Coaching methods	Attend supervisory training program
Training methods	Attend Train the Trainer program
Interviewing methods	Conduct benchmarking study of best practice companies

STEP 4:
DEVELOP CONTRIBUTION PLAN

What to do:

Quarterly contribution plan is developed for current processes and projects, including performance measures for service, speed, quality and cost as defined above. Value-added contribution is determined for each item.

How to do it:

1) Supervisor and staff member meet to discuss current projects and plan project work for the upcoming quarter.
2) Projects for the upcoming quarter are listed on the planning form, along with related performance measures
3) A value-added contribution amount is determined for each item.

Determining Value Added

Organizations add value by gathering inputs (materials, equipment, facilities, staff) and transforming them into outputs that customers are willing to purchase. The amount of total value added is determined as follows:

Value Added = Value of Outputs—Cost of Transformation—Cost of Inputs

Individuals create value added through direct labor on products or services for customers, or by reducing the cost of the transformation process through process improvements such as reduced cost, time, effort and waste.

The value added amount for each project is determined by first assessing if the project involves direct labor or process improvement.

If the project is direct labor, total value added for the project is determined as above. The organization will determine what percent of the value added amount will be shared with employees. The percent amount will vary depending on the level of performance.

If the project adds value through process improvement, the amount of transformation cost savings must be calculated. Percent amounts for reduced costs will be shared, with the amounts varying depending on performance.

Senior Systems Analyst

Contribution	Goal	Value	Result	Date	Reward
Client information requirements	Prepare requirements for XYZ system	25% of project total estimated savings = $2,000			
Computer program design	Complete design for X90 system	50% of project estimated savings = $10,000			
Computer systems development	Complete programming for Customer Information system	30% of savings = $2,500			
Trained Clients	Train clients on Customer Information System	5% of savings = $415			
Total					

Optimal Target % = 30%
Competitive Target % = 20%
Baseline Target % = 10%

Senior Human Resource Representative

Contribution	Goal	Value	Result	Date	Reward
Trained and qualified employees	Reduce average time to fill vacancies from 60 to 45 days	25% of total estimated savings = $1,875			
Delivered staff supplies	Reduce transaction costs by 10%	10% of estimated savings = $1,000			
Accurate payroll	Reduce processing time by 15%	30% of savings = $500			
Total					

Optimal Target % = 30%
Competitive Target % = 20%
Baseline Target % = 10%

STEP 5:
MEASURE PERFORMANCE

What to do:

System for regularly collecting performance data for each contribution is implemented. System provides direct feedback on results to employee (or team).

How to do it:

1) Examine each goal and prepare data collection method and materials for each performance measure.
2) Establish process to gather information as events occur.
3) Have evaluation sheet completed by staff and submitted as each project is complete.

Senior Systems Analyst

Contribution	Goal	Indicator	Result
Client information requirements	Prepare requirements for XYZ system	Speed	125% of estimate
		Quality	Approval after 4 iterations
Computer program designs	Complete design for X90 system	Speed	90% of estimate
		Quality	Exceeds criteria
		Satisfaction	95% satisfaction rating
Computer systems development	Complete Customer Information System	Speed	110% of estimate
		Quality	Criteria met
		Satisfaction	85% satisfaction rating
Trained Clients	Train on Customer Information System	Timeliness	Held 3 days prior to implementation
		Service	Question repeats averaged 2
		Quality	80% Good to Excellent ratings

Senior Human Resource Representative

Contribution	Goal	Indicator	Result
Trained and qualified employees	Reduce average time to fill vacancies from 60 to 45 days	Quality	High retention rate
		Timeliness	Open position rate 3%
		Consistency	Open position rate 3%
Delivered staff supplies	Reduce transaction costs by 10%	Timeliness	.25% not in stock
		Cost	Within budget
		Flexibility	95% appropriate vendor
Accurate payroll	Reduce processing time by 15%	Quality	.5% error rate
		Timeliness	99% deadline met
		Consistency	.5% error rate over time

STEP 6:
DETERMINE PERFORMANCE REWARDS

What to do:

Performance and Development activities are tracked and evaluated as they occur throughout the year. Evaluation includes a full-circle assessment. Rewards, *StaffShare Reward Units* (SRU)©, are earned based on successful performance and value-added contribution. Staff determines how the reward will be delivered - e.g., cash, time-off, added benefits, etc

How to do it:

1) Review evaluation sheet against performance targets as they are submitted.
2) Determine performance level
3) Multiply percent by value to determine SRU
4) Explain SRU redemption options.

Senior Systems Analyst

Contribution	Goal	Value	Result	Date	Reward
Client information requirements	Prepare requirements for XYZ system	25% of project total estimated savings = $2,000	Baseline Targets met	1/15/99	200 SRU
Computer program design	Complete design for X90 system	50% of project estimated savings = $10,000	Competitive Targets met	2/26/99	2000 SRU
Computer systems development	Complete programming for Customer Information system	30% of savings = $2,500	Optimal targets met	3/15/99	750 SRU
Trained Clients	Train clients on Customer Information System	5% of savings = $415	Baseline target met	3/21/99	42 SRU
Total					2,992 SRU

Optimal Target % = 30%
Competitive Target % = 20%
Baseline Target % = 10%

Senior Human Resource Representative

Contribution	Goal	Value	Result	Date	Reward
Trained and qualified employees	Reduce average time to fill vacancies from 60 to 45 days	25% of total estimated savings = $1,875	Competitive Targets met	2/15/00	375 SRU
Delivered staff supplies	Reduce transaction costs by 10%	10% of estimated savings = $1,000	Baseline Targets met	3/15/00	100 SRU
Accurate payroll	Reduce processing time by 15%	30% of savings = $500	Competitive targets met	2/1/00	100 SRU
Total					575 SRU

Optimal Target % = 30%
Competitive Target % = 20%
Baseline Target % = 10%

CONCLUSIONS

The end result of implementing this system in your organization is a customer-focused, results-oriented, learning organization. All systems, from strategy to rewards are in alignment. Responsibility and accountability are clearly defined. Employees understand expectations and have regular feedback on results. Employees can self-correct if performance is below target and can seek guidance from the coach before real problems occur. Everyone shares in the work, and rewards reflect the level of contribution. The power and energy of your high performing employees is unleashed because the system rewards performance and development rather than mediocrity. As employees strive to reach their individual goals, their contributions enable achievement of corporate goals. The workplace of the third millennium will require organizations to be fast, flexible and customer focused. The key will be an empowered workforce. This book provides you with the know-how to change your HR systems and culture to position your organization for the future.

About the Author

Dr. Torkelson is a Partner in Cedar Ridge Consulting. Her experience includes 20 years of professional and managerial experience in human resources, organizational development, information systems, and strategic planning in the finance industry. Dr. Torkelson is a faculty member teaching in the management and human resource areas, and has also managed and produced compensation and benefits surveys. Her career and educational emphasis has been on structuring organizations to maximize the effective use of systems for the purpose of enhancing individual and organizational performance. Dr. Torkelson has a BBA with a specialization in Human Resources from the University of Wisconsin-Madison, an MBA from Edgewood College and a DBA from Nova Southeastern University. She has also received accreditation as a Senior Professional in Human Resources from the Society of Human Resources Management. She can be reached via email at cedarridge@maqs.net

APPENDIX

Interview Guide

Name:_____   Date:_____

Position Title:_____   Unit:_____

Employer:_____   Manager_____

1) Identify the internal and external customers and the products and services each customer expects from the employee (or team).

    - *"What customer groups need your position's products and/or services?"*

    - *"What products and/or services do you provide to each customer group?"*

    - *"What does your position, and the products and services you provide, contribute to the overall success of your company?"*

2) Determine customer requirements for each product or service. These requirements are the contributions the employee (or team) is expected to deliver.
   - *"What expectations or requirements do internal or external customers have for each product or service?"*

   - *"How does your customer describe or define a quality product or service?"*

   - *"How will your customers expectations change in the future?"*

3) Use the information provided to develop six to ten Contribution Statements that:
   - Describe end **products or services** the position provides to customers. (Not activities carried out on the job).
   - Specify the critical contributions from the customer's point of view.
   - Be sure the statements reflect value-added **results**. Value is added by transforming resources (materials, equipment, intellectual capital) into end products or services. Reviewing work, re-doing work or moving work from one place to another typically do not add value.

   Ask: "What do you leave behind when you go home for the day?"

Actual Contribution Statements:

_____

_____

_____

_____

_____

_____

_____

_____

- Check to make sure the contributions encompass all the key aspects of the position. A contribution is considered "key" if it encompasses 5% or more of the total time available for a position during a measurement period.

- Review each contribution statement and estimate how much total effort (in terms of time) is spent on making the contribution

3) Prepare specific measures for each contribution. Critical measures include service, speed, quality and cost. Verify measures with customers and link to organizational strategy.
    a) For each contribution statement, ask the job experts:
        - *"What performance indicators are most critical to meeting customer requirements?"*
        - *Have them consider all of the following indicators:*
Service	Speed
Quality	Cost
Quantity	Timeliness
Consistency	Productivity
Flexibility	Satisfaction
        - Select the 3 most important indicators for each contribution statement

Contribution Statement	Indicator 1	Indicator 2	Indicator 3

b) Determine specific numeric or descriptive measures for each contribution.
- For each indicator selected above, ask:
- *"What could be counted or kept track of to measure this indicator? And "In what units?" (e.g. # errors, % completed, etc)*
- *If a qualitative judgment must be made ask: "Who evaluates this part of the job?" "When this person assesses t*he product or service, what factors should be evaluated?"

Contribution Statement:

Indicator	Measure/Evaluator	Units/Factors

Contribution Statement:

Indicator	Measure/Evaluator	Units/Factors

Contribution Statement:

Indicator	Measure/Evaluator	Units/Factors

Contribution Statement:

Indicator	Measure/Evaluator	Units/Factors

Contribution Statement:

Indicator	Measure/Evaluator	Units/Factors

Contribution Statement:

Indicator	Measure/Evaluator	Units/Factors

Contribution Statement:

Indicator	Measure/Evaluator	Units/Factors

Contribution Statement:

Indicator	Measure/Evaluator	Units/Factors

Contribution Statement:

Indicator	Measure/Evaluator	Units/Factors

Contribution Statement:

Indicator	Measure/Evaluator	Units/Factors

c) Create **Baseline** performance targets for each measure:
- For numeric measures use current average performance. Do not set the baseline below the worst performance for any previous period.
- For descriptive measures determine what the judge would see that meant that expectations had been met.
- For cost measures determine the acceptable cost.
- For cost reduction measures consider what amount of rework or waste is acceptable.

- For timeliness measures determine when the project needs to be completed.
- For speed measures determine how fast the cycle time should be.

d) Create **Competitive** level performance targets. These targets are short-term performance improvement goals. They should be set higher than the current average or typical performance, but not higher than the best performance ever achieved.

e) Create **Optimal** level performance targets. These are long-term performance improvement goals. They are significantly better than current performance, and may be the ultimate level of performance, such as zero errors, or 100% satisfaction.

Contribution Statement	Indicator	Measure	Performance Targets	
			Baseline	
			Competitive	
			Optimal	
			Baseline	
			Competitive	
			Optimal	
			Baseline	
			Competitive	
			Optimal	
			Baseline	
			Competitive	
			Optimal	
			Baseline	
			Competitive	
			Optimal	
			Baseline	
			Competitive	
			Optimal	
			Baseline	
			Competitive	
			Optimal	

4) Determine the essential functions and the knowledge, skills and abilities necessary to deliver the contributions.

a) Functions are the tasks we do in order to accomplish the contributions expected from the position. **Essential functions** represent a summary of the key tasks associated with a job, and are common to all job description formats. Essential functions are used to comply with the Americans with Disabilities Act and will be used in a later step to make market salary comparisons. The essential functions list those duties that *must* be performed in the job.

- Review each contribution statement and determine what must be done on the job to produce the results required by customers. List the appropriate tasks after each contribution statement.

b) Determine which functions are essential. Ask the following questions:

- *"Does the position exist to perform this function?"* For example, when a person is hired to proofread documents, the ability to proofread is an essential function because this is the only reason for the existence of the job.
- *"Is the function highly specialized?"* In highly skilled positions, a worker is hired because they possess special expertise in a particular area. The performance of that specialized task would be an essential function.
- *"Are there a limited number of employees among whom the function can be distributed?"* In this type of situation, functions may become essential that might not be considered essential if there were a larger staff where the work can be more spread out.
- "Would the job be fundamentally altered if you were to remove the function in question?" *If the purpose of the job*

> *would still be accomplished without performing the function, it might not be an essential one.*

- *"What happens if the function is not performed?" If there are no particular consequences for failure to perform the function it might not be essential.*

Contribution Statement:

Task	Essential Function?
	☐ Yes ☐ No
	☐ Yes ☐ No
	☐ Yes ☐ No
	☐ Yes ☐ No
	☐ Yes ☐ No

Contribution Statement:

Task	Essential Function?
	☐ Yes ☐ No
	☐ Yes ☐ No
	☐ Yes ☐ No
	☐ Yes ☐ No
	☐ Yes ☐ No

Contribution Statement:

Task	Essential Function?
	☐ Yes ☐ No
	☐ Yes ☐ No
	☐ Yes ☐ No
	☐ Yes ☐ No
	☐ Yes ☐ No

Contribution Statement:

Task	Essential Function?
	☐Yes ☐No
	☐Yes ☐No
	☐Yes ☐No
	☐Yes ☐No
	☐Yes ☐No

Contribution Statement:

Task	Essential Function?
	☐Yes ☐No
	☐Yes ☐No
	☐Yes ☐No
	☐Yes ☐No
	☐Yes ☐No

Contribution Statement:

Task	Essential Function?
	☐Yes ☐No
	☐Yes ☐No
	☐Yes ☐No
	☐Yes ☐No
	☐Yes ☐No

Contribution Statement:

Task	Essential Function?
	☐ Yes ☐ No
	☐ Yes ☐ No
	☐ Yes ☐ No
	☐ Yes ☐ No
	☐ Yes ☐ No

Contribution Statement:

Task	Essential Function?
	☐ Yes ☐ No
	☐ Yes ☐ No
	☐ Yes ☐ No
	☐ Yes ☐ No
	☐ Yes ☐ No

Contribution Statement:

Task	Essential Function?
	☐ Yes ☐ No
	☐ Yes ☐ No
	☐ Yes ☐ No
	☐ Yes ☐ No
	☐ Yes ☐ No

Contribution Statement:

Task	Essential Function?
	☐Yes ☐No
	☐Yes ☐No
	☐Yes ☐No
	☐Yes ☐No
	☐Yes ☐No

c) Competencies are composed of the underlying knowledge, abilities and skills needed to perform the work that generates results and contributions. As employees increase their competency level, they are more easily able to achieve better results. In addition, increasing competencies helps position the organization to readily adapt in a rapidly changing environment. Growing competencies in a flat organization provides a sense of upward mobility and career development, which aids in retention of growth-motivated staff.

1) Determine the **Knowledge** necessary to accomplish each contribution statement:

    Knowledge is defined as a body of information applied directly to the performance of a function.

    Ask the following questions:

    - *"What subject matter areas are covered by this contribution?"*
    - *"With what facts or principles must the worker have an acquaintance or understand in these subject areas?"*
    - Examples of knowledge statements:

        Knowledge of accounting principles, practices and procedures

        Knowledge of computer science theory and concepts

Knowledge of management principles, practices and procedures

2) Determine the **Abilities** necessary to accomplish each contribution statement:

Ability is defined as a present competence to perform an observable behavior or a behavior that results in an observable product.

Ask the following questions:

- *"What is the nature and level of language ability, written or oral, required of the worker on the job?"*
- *"Are there complex oral or written ideas involved in performing the contribution, or will simple instructional materials suffice?"*
- *"What mathematical ability must the worker have?" "Will the incumbent use simple arithmetic, complex algebra?"*
- *"What reasoning or problem solving ability must the worker have?"*
- *"What instructions must the worker follow?" "Are they simple, detailed, involved, abstract?"*
- *What interpersonal abilities are required?" "What supervisory or managerial abilities are required?"*
- *"What physical abilities such as strength, coordination, visual acuity must the worker have?"*
- Examples of ability statements:

    Ability to research, evaluate and make recommendations

    Ability to conduct training

    Ability to design and write programs in "C"

Ability to design software programs to solve business problems

3) Determine the Skills necessary to accomplish each contribution statement:

Skill is defined as a present, observable competence to perform physical activities associated with mental processes.

Ask the following questions:

- *"What activities must the worker perform with ease and precision?"*
- *"What are the manual skills that are required to operate machines, vehicles, equipment or to use tools?"*
- Examples of Skill statements:

    Skill in the use of a calculator

    Skill in the use of standard tools and equipment

    Skill in the use of keyboards

Contribution Statement:

Knowledge	Ability	Skill

Contribution Statement:

Knowledge	Ability	Skill

Contribution Statement:

Knowledge	Ability	Skill

Contribution Statement:

Knowledge	Ability	Skill

Contribution Statement:

Knowledge	Ability	Skill

Contribution Statement:

Knowledge	Ability	Skill

Contribution Statement:

Knowledge	Ability	Skill

Contribution Statement:

Knowledge	Ability	Skill

Contribution Statement:

Knowledge	Ability	Skill

Contribution Statement:

Knowledge	Ability	Skill

5) Assess the relative value of each knowledge, skill and ability. Rate the KSA's with respect to importance, frequency, and development potential.

Use the guide presented under each category to identify the appropriate level of each Knowledge, Skill or Ability necessary for effective performance.

a) Importance: *"How important is this KSA to effective performance?"*

| Minimal | Moderate | Major |
| Importance | Importance | Importance |

1 ——— 2 ——— 3 ——— 4 ——— 5---- 5

b) Development potential: *"To what extent will increased expertise make a significant difference in performance?"*

| Minimal | Moderate | Major |
| Difference | Difference | Difference |

1 ——— 2 ——— 3 ——— 4 ——— 5---- 5

c) Frequency: *"How often is this KSA used in delivering effective performance?"*

Twice
Yearly Yearly Monthly Weekly Daily Hourly Continually

1 ——— 2 ——— 3 ——— 4 ——— 5 ——— 6 ——— 7 ----- 7

Knowledge, Skill, Ability	Importance	Development Potential	Frequency	Total

6) Prepare definitions of each KSA, and develop benchmark behavioral descriptions showing entry, intermediate and advanced level of expertise.

   a) Determine the domain of the KSA. The domain indicates the scope of the Knowledge, Skill or Ability required by the position under review. For example, a Technical Specialist and a Database Administrator both need to possess knowledge of computer networking, testing and system administration. The domain of the knowledge is different as shown below:

Domain

Knowledge	Technical Specialist	Database Administrator
Computer networking, testing and system administration	Computer connectivity, including cabling, disk and CPU usage, UNIX system commands, troubleshooting errors	Database structure, concepts, software testing methodology, system security issues

   b) Write behavioral descriptions that illustrate how a particular Knowledge, Skill or Ability is demonstrated on the job. Develop benchmarks for individuals just starting out in a position, individuals who have gained experience and expertise to support independent work, and lastly, individuals who are acknowledged experts and idea leaders.

   Individuals possess entry-level KSA's when they

   • Work under the supervision and direction of a more experienced staff member

   • Work products are a portion of a larger project or activity being overseen by an experienced staff member

- Lack experience and status in the organization
- Are expected to willingly accept supervision and direction
- Do most of the detailed and routine work on a project
- Exercise guided creativity and limited initiative
- Are learning to perform well and accomplish a task within the time allowed.

Individuals possess intermediate-level KSA's when they
- Go into depth in one problem or technical area
- Assume responsibility for a definable portion of a project, process or clients
- Work independently and produce significant results
- Develop credibility and a solid reputation
- Rely less on manager for answers and develops own resources to solve problems
- Increases in confidence and ability

Individuals possess advanced-level KSA's when they:
- Make significant contributions in own area of expertise but also contribute in other key areas
- Stimulate others by sharing ideas and information
- Help develop expertise in other staff members through leadership and mentoring roles
- Represents the organization to individuals and institutions outside the organization
- Negotiates and makes commitments for the organization

Example

KSA	Domain	Entry	Intermediate	Advanced
Ability to conduct training	Subject knowledge, presentation skills, adult training techniques, facilitation techniques, composure, credibility	Prepares and presents small group training on familiar and basic processes using established materials. Evaluations indicate room for growth	Prepares and presents large group training and training on more complex subjects. Regularly receives good evaluation ratings from participants	Able to independently prepare and present any type of scheduled or spontaneous training. Consistently receives excellent ratings from participants.
Project management	Planning and applying a methodology to a specific project to reach the desired outcome.	Basic knowledge of project management for small, limited scope projects.	Ability to apply knowledge of project management to all projects.	Knowledge applied to large, complex projects and shares knowledge with project leaders.
Systems analysis	Principles, practices and procedures involved in analyzing business processes to create and improve efficiency of workflow.	Understands basic concepts and methodology. Can independently analyze projects of limited complexity.	Understands how to apply concepts and methods to a wide variety of projects. Works independently.	Innovates based on breadth of knowledge. Provides guidance to others and leads team for complex, critical projects.

KSA	Domain	Entry	Intermediate	Advanced

7) Use the essential functions to make external position comparisons to establish the base pay range for the position. Determine the proportion

of the salary range attributable to performance and that attributable to KSA's.

a) Determine if you wish to conduct your own survey or use existing survey material. This process assumes the use of published survey data.

- Determine the market area for your positions. Market areas may be local, statewide, regional, or national. Markets are likely to vary for positions, with higher level or more technical positions drawing from a larger market area.
- Visit the library to determine what survey data is readily available. Call trade associations, professional societies and government agencies for additional survey resources. Evaluate the resources for applicability to your situation: Determine:
- If any of your former employees left your firm to work for other companies that have participated in the survey.
- If you have hired many employees from the participating companies
- If the survey covers at least some firms that are regarded as competitors.
- If the survey covers companies of similar size to your firm.
- If the survey covers jobs similar to those in your firm.
- If the survey data is dominated by a few particularly high- or low- paying firms.
- Your aim is to select surveys of competitive companies within a relevant geographic area.

b) Review the data that is presented in the survey to ascertain that the rates of pay are clearly defined. Base rates of pay should not include shift differentials, overtime rates or other premium rates

c) Select the jobs in the survey that are similar to those in the firm. To do this, study the brief job descriptions provided with the survey, and compare these brief descriptions to the essential functions you identified.

d) Find the average wage for each job from the survey. The best measure to use is the inter-quartile range, or the middle 50 percent, which is the range of data resulting from discarding the highest 25 percent and the lowest 25 percent of the reported data. The exclusion of the high and low quartiles eliminates from the data trainees and persons who are overpaid, and reduces the mean's sensitivity to extremes. If the inter-quartile range is not available, use the mean.

e) Once you have identified the market wage for each position, you may want to update the information by increasing the data by making a cost of living adjustment based on the change in the Consumer Price Index since the time the data was published.

f) Base salary data reported in surveys includes pay for performance. When paying for contributions, you want base salary to only reflect the core competencies possessed by staff. Therefore, you need to subtract from the market wage an amount that accounts for performance pay.

g) Use your performance appraisal system or judgment to determine:
- Which employees are "superior" performers, defined as those whose performance is better than 85% of their colleagues, and only 15% turn in better performance.
- Which employees are "average" performers
- Which employees are "low performing" employees, defined as those employees whose performance is less effective than 85% of their colleagues, and only 15% turn in worse performance.

- Obtain salary data for employees in each category for each position.
- Calculate an average salary for each category.
- Find the difference between the mean "superior" performer category and the "average" performer category.
- Find the difference between the mean "low performing" category and the "average" performer category.
- Calculate the average of these two differences. This is the performance differential paid in your company.
- Subtract the performance differential from the market wage to establish the competency-based average salary
- Establish the salary range by alternately adding and subtracting 10% to 25% (depending on your firms past practice for salary administration) to and from the average wage.

Printed in the United Kingdom
by Lightning Source UK Ltd.
104738UKS00001B/201